BounceBackAbility

Reclaim Your Power and Passion After Divorce

ZELDA MARSH

First published by Ultimate World Publishing 2020
Copyright © 2020 Zelda Marsh

ISBN

Paperback - 978-1-922372-02-4
Ebook - 978-1-922372-03-1

Zelda Marsh has asserted her right under the Copyright, Designs and Patents Act 1988 to be identified as the author of this work. The information in this book is based on the author's experiences and opinions. The publisher specifically disclaims responsibility for any adverse consequences, which may result from use of the information contained herein. Permission to use information has been sought by the author. Any breaches will be rectified in further editions of the book.

All rights reserved. No part of this publication may be reproduced, stored in or introduced into a retrieval system, or transmitted in any form, or by any means (electronic, mechanical, photocopying, recording or otherwise) without the prior written permission of the author. Any person who does any unauthorised act in relation to this publication may be liable to criminal prosecution and civil claims for damages. Enquiries should be made through the publisher.

Cover design: Ultimate World Publishing
Layout and typesetting: Ultimate World Publishing
Editor: Hayley Ward

Ultimate World Publishing
Diamond Creek,
Victoria Australia 3089
www.writeabook.com.au

Disclaimer

The stories and events in this book are all true to me, the opinions are mine and this is my version.

This book does come with a trigger warning, so please consider how you may react if you're about to read a particular incident or occasion that may open some deep emotional wounds for you.

While I have tried to refrain from using too many names, you will find lots of details. I felt that I needed to convey the real-life feel of the situations I have been in and so decided to keep some of the graphic details in place.

Testimonials

I could say so much about this amazing person; how do I put all of who she is in a short space? Little did I know that when choosing her in an advertisement all those years ago I would find my most treasured, influential and lifetime best friend. Between us, we have been through so many challenges, and I believe she has shown me how to grow.

Zelda has this way of just knowing; she always saw a part of me I never did, she believed in me when I never could, helping me develop into the confident woman I am today that I never was in the past.

Zelda is genuine, compassionate and level-headed. She can always be counted on, offers hard, honest advice and support when needed, and above all whatever else she ever has going on, she listens. Her wonderful sense of humour and adventure with her lifetime experiences have given her the ability to see any given situation in a positive light.

Being on the other side of the world doesn't stall me from knowing that in a heartbeat she will be there if I need her.

Anyone given the chance to get to know Zelda should consider themselves very lucky. Zelda is much more than just a friend, she is one of the truest and best friends ever. Melanie.

M. L. Collis
Director, T E C Inspections Ltd. England

I learned that I am valuable just the way I am. I was very down about my future; both financially and in possible future relationships. I was feeling very rejected by my ex-husband. Now that my self-confidence is better, I can see the possibility of a bountiful future. I now feel inspired to continually grow and have greatly improved my self-talk!

My confidence is much improved and I have grown emotionally. I will continue to work on self-acceptance now that Zelda has given me the tools to help me. I am most proud of my improved view of my looks, and I have also learned that I am a worthwhile human being! I can live alone and be happy! 'The program' was so worthwhile! I'm thankful for Zelda's work with me.

Barrie Ayars Mechanicsburg, PA, USA

Dedication

I wish to dedicate this book to all those bastards who thought they could hurt, ruin and break me.

I owe you so much gratitude for giving me these life experiences that I have managed to use to create the strong, determined woman I am today. Thank you very much, and by the way, how's life treating you?

My babies, Lucy, Thomas and Bobby, for giving me the purpose and strength that's made my life worth living. For accepting our strange, indifferent and chaotic lifestyle.

Mostly for being yourselves and bringing me so much love and pride.

Lucy, you are my mini-me and my rock.

Thomas, for your drive and passion. Continue to follow your dreams.

Bobby, my baby, for massively increasing the population, thanks, can you stop now!

Twinkles, you have opened my eyes to freedom, individuality and acceptance. My husband Geoff, I love you as you, even though you scare the pants off me with your lack of fear – AKA, my Crocodile Dundee. I am not a princess, just English.

My mentors, spiritual teachers and business coaches who between them have allowed me to see my gold as a blessing and purpose instead of reason not to shine by nurturing me and showing me how my vulnerability has become my courage.

My final dedication is to all you beautiful ladies out there who have experienced sadness, loss or pain in the hands of another.

I love you all. Together we can reconnect, bring in love and stop the rest.

Contents

Disclaimer iii
Testimonials v
Dedication vii
Introduction xi
1. The Monster in my Closet 1
2. The Power of Forgiveness 25
3. Detach to Attach 33
4. Reconnect with Self 45
5. Passion and Purpose 57
6. Discovering your Tribe 69
7. Sharing is Caring 83
8. Honouring yourself 97
9. In the Words of my Little Sis 111
10. Freedom to Believe 121
11. Back on the market - the dating game 139
12. This is you 153
Testimonials-Continued 161
Author Bio 165

Introduction

"No one can tell what goes on between a person you were and the person you become. No one can chart that blue and lonely section of hell. There are no maps of the change, you just come out the other side."

Stephen King

Where did BounceBackAbility come from you may be wondering?

I believe it may have started the day I was born; all those horrific events that challenged me through the experiences and dramas throughout my life.

On reflection, this has given me gratitude, my responsible personality and taught me how to create my own survival mode; hence how to bounce back from any ordeal or challenge.

The penny-dropping moment that created the vision of this book didn't start until 50 years to the day after birth - there came the moment of my epiphany or spiritual dream, wakeup call or vision that had occurred on my 50th Birthday.

Laying there reflecting on it I thought 'yeah right', 'as if', and 'fuck that'. No way could I ever write a book nor tell anyone what shit I've been through; this was personal and my own inner crisis.

Notice how I manage to put up the resistance and defence mechanisms straight away?

Don't get me wrong, I've always been a talker; loud and opinionated, a connector with people. People have always been my passion. I love something about everyone; good and bad people all have something to love, just being in the presence of bodies and connecting with their energies. I love to people-watch; I seek out the expressions, the body language and oh my, the eyes. The eyes are definitely the window to the soul, and somehow, I can feel that.

Getting so much joy from helping others in both my personal and business life, in the health and social sector, I have encouraged and inspired many by my thoughts and ideas. I have found purpose and belief for many along the way, and to see what they simply cannot has always been a talent I took for granted. I have always had an innate ability to help others do what they do best, even if they can't see it.

This has brought me to my many stories that I now have to share. I definitely had a story or two up my sleeve, or lots of gold as I was advised on many an occasion, but my stuff was my stuff, I wasn't comfortable letting that go public for anyone, until now.

The book unveils the true purpose of my pitfalls; I was sick and tired of being the target for abuse.

Introduction

I had a lifetime of constant chaos with abuse and hurt and I just couldn't seem to get away from it - and believe me I spent a lifetime trying and searching for the good. I realised I was constantly attracting drama and it was killing me, it really was. If it wasn't for my guides and my inner strength, I know I wouldn't have written this book, and for that I hold gratitude.

So, what on earth was I supposed to write a blooming book about, I wondered?

As I continued on my spiritually-guided path and progressed through my therapies, I remained sat on that until around five months later, a first-time author's workshop appeared on my Facebook feed, and I felt a burning deep inside me to attend.

Wow, I was so inspired to do this. I had no idea how or what the overall book would consist of apart from my life and spiritual journey.

I never anticipated it bringing me to what BounceBackAbility really is and all it stands for.

It is a true reflection of me and my golds.

It's a book filled with determination, responsibilities, forgiveness, growth, survival, love, humour, foul language, overcoming life situations, mistakes, families, standing up for others, divorce, and doing whatever it takes to get back up and stand up for what you believe to be right for you.

The reason I wrote this book, I believe, is because my purpose is to get the message of hope, love, belief and all of the above out to you. I want you to know you are not alone, and you really do not need to hide your truths. I want to share my stories and show you how not to do it, with ways on how you can do it.

BounceBackAbility

To each of you beautiful people out there in search of answers and inspiration to take no more and do whatever it takes, to make you stand up and be happy, including learning to love yourselves.

Much love, Zelda

The Monster in my Closet

It is estimated that approximately 1% of the general male population are psychopaths, 15 to 20 % of the prison population are psychopathic, 2.2 million Australians have experienced domestic violence and 3.6 have experienced emotional abuse.[1]

There I lay, on my brother's grave, screaming, begging and pleading with him to take me to him.

The last straw

I would do absolutely anything right now to be dead, because I knew I had to die as living this life was far too painful to continue. Reliving those words, I still feel those strong sensations of pain rushing through to my very soul, all my cells and deep in my guts.

---

[1] Online publication in the journal legal and criminological psychology

BounceBackAbility

This was a place I would never wish to return to, nor do I want any other human being in the world to have to sink that low and feel this through the actions of another.

Don't get me wrong, it needed me to get there, to understand that I had to do something. I had to start listening to all those freaking signs I had been getting for far too long now. I mean, loving someone and wanting to do something, anything, to get them better had to come at a better cost, surely? Well, for me, it definitely did.

It was a wakeup call and following the aftermath of leaving and learning far too many lessons I have never looked back. So, I'm actually grateful to have met the monster that drove me to attempting suicide, because the life I have created for myself since then has brought me freedom for the first time, in a way no one would know unless they've been trapped or imprisoned before.

The time I hit the pit was only two months after we had a party to celebrate our engagement. Even that nearly didn't happen - and shouldn't have. What on earth were we thinking? I'm not denying I was crazy in love at the time and wanted the loving, sexy side of this gorgeous man, but not the side of him that began to show up as often as the monster side by then.

I understood what Dr Jekyll and Mr Hyde was all about by now. The relationship was toxic. I couldn't breathe, never had a moment to myself, and I was suffocating. When he was working away out at sea for a month at a time, he would call and message me all day and night long. Each day was at least three hours of conversation or fallouts because he didn't want to be there, he wanted to be home with me. Yes, at first I was flattered; I actually believed that he loved me so much it was killing him being apart from me. Little did I know at the time what was really going on. Even when he was home, I just thought he was overly passionate and again I believed he just couldn't get enough of me. I was flattered that a man could finally show me all this affection.

When it was good it was absolutely mind-blowing. I would be treated like a princess. He would show me love, affection, attention, wear me on his arm with pride. I felt amazing. I felt like his queen and thought I had finally found the man of my dreams. I certainly wouldn't even consider looking at another man, even though I was battling with the red mist days; questions and accusations that were constantly wearing me down, yet I only saw the good and ignored the bad.

Talk about humiliation

One day I was at home and he walked in, swung me around and kissed me passionately then asked me where my leather gloves were. I told him they were on the passenger seat of my car. England in the winter is cold so I drove with my leather gloves. He asked me if I was sure. Of course I was, I had worn them earlier that day. He wanted me to check, so I humoured him as I often had to. I was already becoming anxious because he had that look in his eyes that only meant one thing to me those days (the red mist has hit). There was only one glove on the seat. He asked me where the other one was. Well, obviously it was there earlier. I searched the whole car, the driveway, my bag, as well as the whole house, just in case I had picked it up and dropped it on the way in.

Here came the questions - who had I had in my car; did I have the guy I mentioned from work a few days earlier? I was a care coordinator at the time and we had an induction that had a male care worker on it. I may have mentioned this in a passing conversation about my day and it obviously got mixed up with his mental state. As much as I kept telling him no one had been in my car he was insistent and kept going on and on about this missing glove. He stated I must have used this glove as a sexual reference with this man.

Obviously, I hadn't, and I had no explanation as to where my glove had gone. I was forced to call my office after hours to ask if a glove had been handed in. Talk about humiliating. After hours was only supposed to be called for emergencies, so I felt really unprofessional calling in for this. To make it worse, he asked to me to get them to check the CCTV to see if someone had broken into my car or got in if I may have forgotten to lock it in the day. After that I had to tell him what this man's name was, which broke all the confidentiality policies, however, my fear took over and I gave him the name. He got my phone and searched all the men under that name on Facebook until he found him.

Then he gave various scenarios of us together and said he was going to message him and threaten to kill him. I got that all night, he got drunk and I had no sleep, terrorised with accusations and a smashed phone because I wouldn't add him as a Facebook friend. I'm not sure how long this went on for but I do remember a few weeks later my glove reappeared in our porchway and I was accused of planting it there. I believe he had taken the glove before he got in the house that night and planned the entire façade of terrorism on me again.

Planting the seed again

I say again because this sort of behaviour was increasing, and it wasn't funny in the least. On another occasion we were living at his mum's house and my bestie had come around for a cup of tea. I hadn't seen much of her lately and I knew she could always read me, so I had to be careful. While I was downstairs catching up, he had gone upstairs for a shower, and I thought nothing unusual at the time. It wasn't until she left that I went upstairs to our room and he was acting the red mist way again, saying my phone had been ringing and ringing while I was downstairs. I checked my phone and it had a few missed calls from an unknown number. I asked why he didn't answer it for me as I was downstairs, and he said because he didn't want to talk to my boyfriend. Here we go again, I thought to myself. So, he made me ring the number and it didn't answer. I asked him to ring it so he did, then later texts came through from one of his best friends making out he was there for me if 'the monster was playing up'. I said I was fine thank you and he didn't need to call me.

This continued into the night and I was awoken in the night after I thought we were both asleep to cold beer being poured over my head (another thing that became a habit of his). When I couldn't answer whatever was going on in his mind, I would get thrown off the bed, a pillow squashing my head hard into the ground until I could hardly breathe. I can't tell you how many times this happened or how many times I ran out of the house crying and screaming, with him trying to drag me back inside. I felt safer sitting outside in the garden in the cold or rainy nights than being thrown around the house like a ragdoll.

When the red mist had kicked in, he never remembered what he had done or said, then I'd get a few quiet days where he would feel sorry for himself; not for what he did or said to me, he was just beating himself up over it.

Seeing stars

I understood the phrase seeing stars because when your head is banged hard enough into the ground that's exactly what you do - see stars. I hid bruises, I lied to my own children and his mother about the bruises I couldn't hide or didn't realise were there.

I lied and I lied and I lied, not just to myself, but whenever he asked me to cover him over nothing much to his mum, he'd come back later and go mad at me for lying. I lied to the police when they came around looking for him and asking if I was ok. I lied at the hospital when he kicked me to the ground and I was taken by paramedics to find I had a fractured sacrum, I wouldn't give his name and he went mad at me because he had smashed my phone again and couldn't get hold of me.

I just couldn't compete with his mind or mentality.

Devasted

My granddaughter's christening was supposed to be a wonderful occasion. Firstly, my son rang me after the ceremony that I missed because I was given the wrong time and I was supposed to be going on my own just in case an ex of mine was there. But he decided last minute he was coming. He was tormenting me about the guests and the fact that the ex was there, so I kept away and acted like I was fine. He approached the ex and was playing up to him and buying him drinks, then coming and whispering things like he was going to kill him, so he got drunk. Then arguments started over nothing to do with us as it happened, however, we got thrown out and I left him. Again, I was devastated by another humiliation - I had enough.

This night was a night I'll never forget for as long as I shall live. Back at home, I was packing to leave when he arrived. He was shoving cocaine up his nose and goading me about the ex - nothing else, just him. This ex was three years before I had even met the "monster," but he was obsessed by him because he was a lot younger than me, so he saw him as a threat, for no reason at all. I would get woken many a night terrorised with Facebook images and he'd be stalking him and telling me what he'd do to him if he got hold of him, as well as smash my face and throw alcohol on me, blah blah blah.

This night was the worse, he wouldn't let it go. His red mist was the worst I had ever seen it. He locked me in the bedroom and had music blaring. He had taken his belt out of the room and said he was going to hang himself. I heard the attic steps being pulled down, so I panicked.

I have no idea where I got the strength, but I managed to break the lock on the door and get out. I went up to the attic and there he was hanging off the rafters by his belt. I was screaming, panicking and crying, pulling the belt loose. He wasn't responding, and I thought he was dead.

He wasn't, and he pulled the belt off me to have another go, but I grabbed it and hid it. He came back with the dog lead and tried again. I hid anything that looked like it could be used. This went on for many hours. I was locked in the house.

He couldn't get anything inside, so he went out to use the washing line, then stood on top of the garage, threatening to go again. In the meantime, I had found his phone and tried to call his cousin to help him, but soon discovered they had the same behaviour; there was no answer.

When I came out and saw him up there, I was exhausted and couldn't take anymore, so I just screamed, "If you're going to do it, then do it, I'm not standing here and watching you."

I ran like crazy, barefoot down the dark streets, running in alleyways, hiding behind people's back gardens. In fact, I slept, huddled up in an alleyway for a while. At one point I heard him close by, then sneakily a few hours later I got into my sister's back garden (my house that she was renting from me at the time - he wouldn't live there because someone else had shared it with me before). I sat there until she woke up and saw me. I couldn't move and I daren't breath. She took photos of me which were later used as evidence. I didn't tell her what happened or what I was going through. I stayed for a few days until he won me over again.

A name for the shame

It was just after that I started to get personal messages from friends and colleagues asking if I had bruises on my face. Obviously, I denied I had.

I had been to visit a friend for her birthday. She didn't know what had been going on, but as soon as I arrived, she guessed something because she knew me enough to see the changes in me; the changes and scars I thought I had hidden so well.

She managed to get me to think about what I was doing and to look at the state of myself. I gave it a lot of thought that weekend. I wondered how I could move on from living in his dark shadows, but not only that, I was hooked, madly in love and I could only see the pain it would cause, not only me but to him too. Not to mention having to admit what had been happening - I was far too proud and too damn ashamed to let anyone know what I was allowing him to do this to me. I'd always claimed that no man would ever treat me this way, as I was a strong, independent and confident woman, so how could I let them see this?

There's a name many of us get, and not just **victim**, which was the one word I refused to be labelled with at the time.

Another name is a variation of the Stockholm syndrome. I don't believe this is isolated to hostage victims, but to anyone who has been involved in any traumatic relationship - either falling for the abuser, already in love or in a relationship with them!

Ok, there's narcissist, psychopath, sociopath and many more names for them, yet that's irrelevant. What is relevant is that when you are at the mercy of a lover or abuser you can't just walk away, especially when you are bonded and connected; it's impossible to just leave them. You become fearful of what may happen to them before you fear what will become of you. That is the sad reality.

Hitting the pits

After beating myself up for the next few days, I felt partly free yet also partly yearning to get home. I had decided it was in my best interest not to go back to him, even though we had still been messaging and talking to each other throughout the weekend and I gave no sign to him that I would leave.

I stopped off at four different shops and bought some painkillers - in England you're only allowed two packets at a time. Then I bought two litres of alcohol and drove to my brother's grave.

That resulted in me drunk and overdosed, being collected and put in his van (another regular thing I became accustomed to was if I tried to escape him he'd drive around looking for me and throw me in the van or on a few occasions drive me towards a family member's home and I'd jump out and try and run off, until he caught me again).

I had drunk-text him that I wasn't coming home, I was having a drink with my brother! I ended up throwing up all over the place, getting bathed and videoed in this condition too, which I found out later as he showed me with pride. And as I lay in my room for a few days - in and out of consciousness - he acted like it was all a joke; he even joked to his cousin.

A lesser attempt to end the pain

There had been an occasion that we met up and stayed away for the weekend in the caravan. He had persuaded his stepdad to drive it to a location nearer to my city of work, as I was on call. The signal was so poor, I was under pressure already, and to top it off I was anxious because I could sense his mood turning towards the red mist throughout the course of the day as he had been drinking all day. Sure enough, he got off the train with his monster face, the one that the red mist brings.

Immediately anxious, I knew exactly how this weekend would turn out. This time he kept goading me and wanting a fight, but I never wanted that. I always tried to reassure him and reason with him through conversation. It never worked, obviously.

He wouldn't give up and it was never over anything real. Trying to get away from his constant pushing , some hours later I couldn't take anymore so I ran and hid in the dark behind a bush, crying silently, waiting for him to fall asleep, even though I knew damn well he could stay awake for days, especially in this mood. I saw him riding around and he fell off his bike and looked like he had seriously hurt himself, so, like an idiot I went running to his aid. As you may guess, there was no injury; he got me back and started over.

He had used my phone and called my sister a few times. Luckily, she didn't answer as it was in the early hours of the morning by now. He dragged me in the van and started driving towards our hometown, off his face with alcohol and cocaine. I was pleading with him not to involve her or any of my family. I managed to jump out of the van at a village and ran around the streets like some crazy bitch on the loose.

He caught me and promised to take me back to the caravan, which he did, and it got a whole lot worse. This time it got physical. Usually it was just mental torture until he went too far or, I don't know, maybe he didn't get the right reaction or enough attention.

This night, I couldn't cope anymore. While in bed I tried to slice my wrists. Look, I'm no expert but let me tell you, trying to cut yourself without letting on, plus feeling the pain as you cut, fucking hurts and it's hard work. I still kept trying yet hiding it when you're constantly being watched or monitored doesn't help matters.

All I could think is that the pain is still less, and if I do this in my sleep, I won't have to put up with this any longer. I failed.

Falling on deaf ears

That didn't work. I had to return to work and have a meeting with my manager, which was a waste of time. I confided in him what had happened to me, and what I had done. I showed him my wounds and he seemed sympathetic. He made a few notes then did nothing. He thought I was a threat to his role so wasn't very accommodating where I was concerned, however, I actually believed telling someone in power would make a difference. I continued to work and managed to cover up the best I could with bandages, bracelets and long sleeves.

Knowing no one was going to help me when for the first time I actually admitted to someone the truth, made me feel more isolated.

I was alone, battling independently. Even writing this now hurts me and reminds me of how much pain I was living at the time. I believe this is why I need to tell it how it really was, to continue my own healing and work through the triggers.

I left that job after 11 years because of the monster and the manager. No one had a meeting with me to ask why I was leaving, it was just accepted and that hurt; this office, organisation, all of this place was my family, they were my solace my survival portal, my life, and now I was losing everything around me.

I'm never going to unveil all of the horror stories that occurred throughout our relationship and I don't need to. It wasn't always that bad, there really were some beautiful times too, otherwise I wouldn't have gone through all that.

Be afraid

After we got together, I found out he had been in prison for football violence. It was near the end that I would learn the reality of how graphic the violence was, and other stories of violent attacks to follow, involving him and a few of his family members that would make anybody afraid. Some of the things he's told me under the influence I wanted to believe he couldn't or wouldn't ever do, yet the reality taught me differently and I'm grateful I got away alive.

He was a clever, devious and mentally unstable man who needed a lot of help. Help I was in no position to give him. I tried and tried to get him professional help. He willingly came along - we went to doctors, help groups, hypnotherapy, the mental health hospital. They sedated him, and he slept. I remember feeling so relaxed in that moment at the hospital. He lied to them all when questioned about being violent towards me, and I stayed quiet.

There was always a reason for his mists.

The last one was just after I met up with my mother properly after around 30 years of an on-off relationship. It was at a new year party with lots of family members, and it was to be a huge thing for me. Soon after we arrived, my mother was joking and laughing with my cousin about some young man. I literally saw the switch flick in him, and the red mist face came on.

I still tried to enjoy and reconnect with my mother and family, and it was mostly going well. I managed to have a conversation with Mum and we got upset, which was fine, but he wasn't happy with that so raised his voice and my mum's man stood up and I thought there was going to be a fight. Thankfully there wasn't, and we eventually went home.

Pushed too far

I got into my nightwear and came downstairs to an angry monster; all he could talk about was the comment made by two people he didn't know which was nothing to do with us. This resulted in him stamping on my phone and pushing my head - or should I say, face - through the double-glazed back door. The glass shattered and there was blood and glass everywhere.

I didn't know exactly what was cut; I daren't look at first in fear of the worst. I found that it was on the bridge of my nose near my right eye; an open wound. He wouldn't let me go to the hospital, because how would I explain it? So, I just got a wet flannel and moulded the flap of skin back in place and held it there tightly all night. I wasn't allowed to call anyone for help or leave the house to go to hospital or anywhere else for that matter, so there I was imprisoned again.

He hid my phone and keys, cleaned up all the glass and put some cardboard over the window. Clearing up and hiding his mess was something he found pride in. It was quite mesmerising. He was so melodic with it too, until he came down and became the victim; that seeker of sympathy and reassurance again afterwards.

I recall being numb and petrified the next morning. My sister had left her phone at my mum's house the night before and he had agreed to drop it off, so he delivered it to her like nothing was wrong, leaving me locked in the house. I know I could have quite easily escaped somewhere; I could have walked to the police station or the hospital, yet that would incriminate him and I felt I needed to keep protecting him.

While he was gone, his mum and stepdad came to the door. I hid from them. I can't tell you how many times I'd wished I'd just opened the door and let them in to see what had happened. Who knows how that may have changed things all around? However, I didn't, I just hid.

A big part of me often thought he wanted to get caught and taken away for help, as I knew he wasn't strong enough to make that decision himself. I certainly wasn't brave enough to do it at the time.

Becoming the victim

Returning to work a few days later with the obvious face injury meant another lie had to come out my mouth. I was now an expert liar so made out I had been bitten by a dog on new year's eve, and it was my own fault because I went to kiss it and it bit me. I could tell that no one really believed me this time but didn't say a word.

During that first day back, he called me and asked if anyone had said anything. I told him what lie I had given them and he went really mad at me for lying again. I asked him if he wanted me to tell them the truth and he said , "don't be stupid, obviously not, what are people going to think of me if they knew I'd done that to you? But look how easy it was for you to be a liar!"

So, I seriously couldn't ever get it right. Even knowing that everything I did was to protect him wasn't good enough. I was never going to be good enough. No matter that through the relationship I had been head-banged, strangled, suffocated, punished, humiliated, tormented, tortured, isolated, kidnapped, deceived, tried to harm myself many times, and pushed to the point of suicide, I was still not good enough.

At work that week I was attending our annual refresher courses on 'POVA', 'Protection of Vulnerable Adults 'and 'Health and Safety', and as the days passed it became worse for me. I sat going through each section on abuse and all of it became about me; I began to feel like the victim that I was.

The final training day arrived. I made a phone call with a friend; she was concerned, and she had heard through a work colleague that I had an injury and knew how strong-willed I could be so wasn't about to open up about it. She said her door was always open for me and I would be safe there. Those words hit me like no others in such a long time.

I had to do something, and it had to be today, so I text my best friend Mel and asked her to come and pick me up from the office and drive me to the doctors. I couldn't take my own car as he often drove past to check where I was. At the doctors, I broke down. I just said I had some problems at home and needed some time off work. I was highly anxious, so she prescribed me some anti-depressants and a sick note for two weeks. Her parting words to me were, "if you need to come back and discuss further, please do and I can refer you to a professional."

"A professional," I thought, "what is she talking about?"

I went to my friend's house to breathe for a bit and consider my options; this was where I learnt about **Clare's law**. My bestie had made some enquiries on my behalf, as this is what the law allows - people to find out if their partner or someone close to their partner has a history of domestic violence. It is intended to provide information that could prevent someone from being a victim of attack. This was that moment when I was given the truth about his violent past. I wasn't alone. I really had no more options; I had to go.

The escape

I text "the monster" to let him know I would go home and check the dog at lunchtime, so he didn't need to. All was well. I was a bag of nerves. I quickly grabbed a bag of clothes and some toiletries. I was so scared he'd come home and catch us there or one of his family would see my friend's car at our place and contact him. I was driven back to my car at the office. I left her my sick note and kissed, hugged and thanked her before I set off and drove all the way to Bradford to a safe place at my friend's home.

This was the beginning of a living nightmare. I arrived safely but my head was a mess. It wasn't long before the reality kicked in and the messages, threats and torments started. The details go too deep, but it ended with me informing the police of his plans to kill himself in a hotel room and waiting to see the fucked up lives he's going to cause when the cleaners find him tomorrow! I knew he meant it; he had sent me photos of the noose he had ready and all the alcohol and drugs he was fuelling himself with, on top of all the details of the how's and whys. I couldn't live with myself knowing his plan.

I managed to work out which hotel he was at. The police discovered him in time then took him to a mental hospital. I felt relieved for him, the hotel staff and for myself - in that order.

The local police had become involved; it was out of my hands and the police had taken the lead. They had suggested this would be a perfect time to drive back - two and a half hours - to collect more of my belongings, and they would arrange with my local police to be there at the other end.

Lizzie would drive me there late at night. Halfway there we got a call; the mental hospital had released him, so he was free. How on earth he managed to convince them he was of sound mind was beyond me; actually, it wasn't as I had become accustomed to his clever and cunning ways.

Once I asked if I could go to my house while he was held at the local police station for his daily check-ins. The police officer said she would need to call her supervisor to check it was ok, and she called me back and said she had asked the monster instead and he said he wanted to be there! Whose side was she on, anyway, I thought. This later became a complaint to the head commissioners of the police who told me she got a slapped wrist and the department would learn by this - oh wonderful, yet again someone will learn something at my expense!

I refused to attend court as I was afraid to see him, and I had asked not to be named because I needed to keep this away from everyone

I knew, especially my sons. I had to work harder to protect them now; if they knew how I had been treated they weren't the type of boys to sit back and do nothing, so I couldn't risk them knowing because only I knew what he was capable of and I'd already had the threats of them being put in body bags before now.

He got away lightly, it appeared in the local papers, and I was named – making out I had been the bad one, of course.

Who was I?

I lost count of the amount of statements I had to give and how many meltdowns I went through. I felt like I was going crazy!

At Lizzie's house, I went through days not sleeping, even taking prescribed sleeping pills that made my mouth taste vile the next day, so I had days of not moving out of the bed - the bed that was in a room with my new room buddy, a then seven-year-old boy, William. Bless him, I'm not sure he ever understood what was going on with Aunty Zelda, who he often referred to as Cinderella or Cinder Rocker Fella.

Now experiencing OCD, I had to keep moving and that meant cleaning and taking care of all the household duties at Lizzie's house! She had no complaints, bless her. Lizzie and her husband Paul would come home and go to a cupboard to look for something and I'd rearranged them. They were so patient with me, they became my saviours, life savers in fact - after all they fed me, clothed me, cared for me, nurtured me, entertained me and the local police force. I had taken over their peaceful life.

My biggest reality check was during one statement I had to give with Lizzie; half the time I couldn't think or stop crying or even admit openly to what they were asking I'd had done to me, let alone answer their constant questions. I do recall, however, being asked what type of person I was before I met "the monster". I don't know, I thought I was just me.

Then listening to Lizzie talk about how the confident, independent, responsible, yet carefree and fun-loving beautiful woman I was had turned into this shell of a woman with no life or light in her eyes anymore, how I had isolated myself and didn't contact or socialise with any of my friends or family anymore; no one knew me, yet everyone was worried.

Then I thought about those few words amongst many more to follow, and she was right - what the fuck had I turned into, and how had I not seen this? Furthermore, why had nobody else told me? What a freaking mess my life was. What a rollercoaster. The one thing I didn't want to be called was a victim, never in my life and certainly not now.

Three months on, I decided I couldn't keep living in this state; dependant on my new family. I gave it a lot of consideration. I knew I couldn't return to my hometown, my family, my friends, my career, my home and all my belongings as they were no longer mine- he had smashed everything up, according to the police.

I decided I needed to get some kind of normality and independence back. I saw an advert for a job as a live-in personal assistant for spinal injured individuals (buy myself some time until I knew where I wanted to base myself). I had years of experience with vulnerable adults of all different levels of disabilities, so I figured this would be a great start for me to move forward.

I had to borrow money to get to the week-long induction near London for food and travel. This job became the biggest and best life-changing decision I had made. I made some new friends, met some wonderful people and visited places I'd never even heard of. On top of that, I was travelling the country and getting money to live; this certainly got me through some very difficult times. Don't get me wrong, I was crying daily and struggling to adapt to all the time I had on my hands, especially between clients. It gave me a lot of thinking time; time I needed.

Funny how life turns around when we allow it to. I started to discover a lot about myself. I learnt what freedom felt like and I knew what feeling alive and breathing was again. I found I was looking back over my shoulder less and less often. I got a statement tattoo to give me constant reminders of my escape and to continue to follow my own dreams from now on. I had to learn to start listening to my intuition for once.

How it started

The first time I ever met 'the monster', I was on a girl's night out. I hadn't long broken up with someone. He was a bundle of life on the dancefloor and he looked playful, charming, fun and gorgeous.

This 6'2" tall, dark and handsome man approached me and was dancing around me to get my attention. Wow! I was very flattered as I thought he was too good to be true to want to dance with me. In my eyes he'd ticked all the boxes for what I would ever want in a man. However, he was cocky and too full of himself, so I elbowed him off, saying, "I don't think so!"

He followed that with, "I'm gonna marry you one day".

"Yeah, of course you are darling", I said, and moved away. I was captured right there and then. He entered my head so many times - there was something mesmerising about him.

It was a month later before I set eyes on him again. It was in the same bar – more dancing. This time I took his phone and instead of giving him my number I added myself on his Facebook and said I'd meet him later. I didn't. The following morning, I had messages from him, and it went from there. In that week we set our first date - I was so nervous!

I was out with some friends and he was to meet up with us. I remember sitting with a group of friends waiting for him to arrive and on the dot in he walked and his smile lit up the entire place. I stood up to let him know where I was. He came over and grabbed me like some romantic movie scene and kissed me there and then. Those lips of his were unforgettable!

He turned around and said, "didn't you say you were single?" I said, "yes" and he followed with, "well you're not now".

And that was it, the start of that passionate, deeply connected, very toxic relationship.

Why you need to leave

The benefits to me leaving were endless, and if you find yourself wondering if you're needing to leave someone right now, consider your own relationship for a moment. Do you feel completely at ease without walking on eggshells? Do you feel happy with who you are and who you are with? Do you feel safe? Does he allow you to be yourself?

When I moved away, I felt alive on good days until eventually it was every day. Passion filled my every cell. I came away from this realising that no matter what I tried to do, I couldn't help, save or heal everyone.

It took me losing absolutely everything for me to permit myself to start a brand-new life. Living in fear allowed me to appreciate that feeling and understanding of real freedom; I discovered that life really was worth living after all.

Things you'd tell yourself now

I've decided to only add a few choice questions for this area. It's a touchy subject and I've had plenty of my share on both sides of the fence on this one.

"I keep getting drawn to his charm."

Of course, you do, but just remember the charm is superficial and as difficult as it is, don't fall for the crap. If he's a narcissist or a psychopath then he knows what strings to pull and what buttons to press, and I assure you they will stop at nothing to get their fix.

"But I love him, he has a really lovely side to him that no one else sees."

I have no doubts he has a lovely side; otherwise why would you have chosen him in the first place? But the reality is, yeah, he's so lovely he manages to use his magic to lure you in to make all the bad in him disappear, hey presto and you become the victim he needs again. Open your eyes darling, it's not real.

"How could I possibly manage my life without him?"

I really do understand why you feel this way, but look around, you haven't actually got a good life have you, and if he is nasty or toxic to the point you're going to get pushed and pushed, you'll not have a chance of a life at all anyway. So, my real answer is you have all the possibilities of living, full stop! Live for yourself, you shouldn't need a man or anyone else for you to live. Let me assure you, with some support, healing work and time you will be amazed at how much of a freaking amazing life you can have!

- ❖ Know your worth and value yourself enough to make the choice to live a safe and happier life.

- ❖ Please keep your friends/family/support network in the know of anything unhealthy or unpleasant, however humiliating or embarrassing you think it may be at the time. Talk to someone, even if it's the Samaritans, DV units or other helplines. Don't withdraw or isolate yourself.

- ❖ Don't be too afraid to sleep.

- ❖ Look out for the red flags/signs - take notes and look back at small changes.

- ❖ Suicide is not the answer, as much as it may seem it at the time.

- ❖ I urge you to check on your friends or family and if you do suspect anything, find a way to connect, you just may be saving a life.

Helplines

Clare's Law (especially if you've been in a toxic relationship or do not know much about a new partner's past). I absolutely say value yourself enough to care and check him out first. (UK)

White Ribbon Australia - awareness against violence towards women. (AU)

1800 RESPECT (on smartphones) 1800737732

Women's aid/refuge (UK) 0808 2000 247

DAME - Domestic Abuse and Money Education

Institute of Justice (USA) 800-799-7233 (SAFE) 800-787-3224 (TITY)

Lifeline - suicide or crisis-13 11 14

Daisy – a smartphone App that connects to local resources and safety procedures

> *Did you know a staggering 65% of divorcees never forgive their ex-partner for the breakdown of their relationship[2]? I find that incredible to take in. Don't get me wrong, I've been one of those myself in the past, but, wow, more than half of you or us will be here right now, so let's see what we can do to change that.*
>
> *According to Wikipedia, forgiveness is an intentional and voluntary process by which a victim undergoes a change of feeling and attitude regarding the offense.*
>
> *Forgiveness is a conscious, deliberate decision to release feelings of resentment or vengeance towards a person who has harmed you.*

---

[2] Psychology today.com

The Power of Forgiveness

"It's not what you eat that makes you sick, its what's eating you that does the sickening."

Unknown

Forgiveness doesn't mean you're condoning, justifying or forgetting what has been done to hurt you. Nor does it mean that someone was right for what they did to you or even what they put you through that caused all the pain you've had in the past.

Consider forgiving

What it does mean, however, is that you accept the shit that happened and allow yourself the chance to move forward with your life. I say 'move forward' rather than 'moving on' because for some people, you'll never move on or even need to. Some of the people who have caused you harm or pain still need to remain in your life, so it's often a necessity, that's when we just move forward with forgivingness, which is often even harder to do.

Hey, let's face it, you can't change the past, so why hang on to it so much?

Doing this is for your own growth and happiness and allows you to live a decent life, without hanging or holding on to anyone that doesn't fit into the life you want for yourself. What you can do is choose how to move forward and how you want your future to look. Start by accepting yourself and making you your highest priority; only then will you make life so much easier for yourself by forgiving someone.

Picture this - no more feeling angry or bitter and just taking in that sense of freedom to move forward with your life once you've removed all that weight off your shoulders. Looks good, doesn't it?

Do you know the health consequences you place on yourself whilst hanging on to pain and memories? Your health while living a life of unforgiveness, I assure you is not pretty – the stress of it can damage your heart. Think about all that deep-rooted pain you're holding onto; what do you think this is going to do to you long term? Anger itself creates stress and anxieties that can lead to depression or social isolation, then this too could lead you to become an outcast, and quite often this can and does lead to heart failure, or even worse, death or suicide, like I tried.

And what do you think harming yourself is doing to them? Nothing. They don't care. They don't feel or even realise what you're doing so take a step back and realise you're only hurting yourself. I know that sounds harsh but it's true; you really do need to consider this forgiveness stage after a divorce. If you don't, you'll stay stuck exactly where you are and who you are right now, unable to move forward with your life with a light heart, struggling to sleep properly which then creates other health deteriorations. Oh, while you're on a roll, you'll allow anger to manifest and fester in all of the other areas of your life too.

Hanging onto anger, resentment, pain, sadness and bitterness has a knock-on effect with all other relationships in your life too, are you really prepared for that? Do you really want to go around feeling resentful of other people's happiness? Do you want to be bitter or twisted every time someone mentions a name or spends time with someone you're allowing to make you feel that way, a trigger that gives you that feel, you know that hot area that gives you that burning pain of fire that eats you alive on the insides? I hope your answer is a big fat no!

Surrendering

Forgiveness will free you up to live in the present. You'll know you're there when you no longer feel contempt, resentment, anger or wish to seek revenge. I say forgive, whether they deserve it or not. It doesn't matter - just do whatever it takes to get rid of the negative emotions that you're storing inside of you for no other purpose than to punish yourself.

For me, forgiveness has placed a heavy burden in my life. I didn't even know where to start or who even deserved my forgiveness, because for a lot of years there were far too many to choose from. Let's face it, in almost 50 years and with a whole lot of nasty situations and so many people to forgive, that wasn't going to happen overnight, or any time soon. I mean, you don't just uncover all these hidden memories and shocking revelations that had been pigeonholed for so long, to then just what, sit back and say, "Oh, it's ok, I forgive you all". Nah, that shit's not real.

What I did do, however, was not allow any grudges or resentment to hold me back from living the best I could under the circumstances. I chose to not allow those bastards to win - being abused in my own home by babysitters and abandoned one way or another by my parents, losing my siblings, step relations abusing me, men thinking they have full access to me and ownership of my body, financially, mentally, emotionally and physically abusing me. Bullied throughout my schooling, workplaces taking liberties, friends abusing my trust, or taking advantage of my skills for free.

The list continues, and it certainly warrants a whole lot of forgiveness, right? I also decided very early on in my life that I never wanted to be seen as a victim or even be seen as vulnerable, however the reality of it all is, I actually was very much both.

As you can see, there's a whole lot of forgiveness to be had. And that's exactly what I did and continue to do today - forgive. Who am I forgiving the most, you may ask?

Well, that is myself.

Once I had discovered I needed to do this for myself, then to do some self-development work, then to proceed to teach others to do the same thing, I mean talk about practicing what I don't preach! Not me, I don't do that, I would never ask anyone to do anything I haven't done myself, or that I wasn't prepared to do either.

I had to work out who I had to forgive and why. I learnt an awful lot about myself and how I had actually attracted all these abusers - ok not as a child, but my childhood had definitely played a massive role in attracting them as an adult. I decided to take control of what I wanted my life to be. I also believe the universe has always had my back, with my spiritual guides that have followed me through my journey, given me the strength and inner power to survive, let alone help me get me through all those turmoils and still hold on to the belief of a happy, meaningful ending. I can't explain it, I just knew, I always felt a presence somehow and do you know what, it doesn't even matter that I didn't even understand what was with me, I just felt comfort in knowing I had something there with me.

What works for me

Meditation plays a daily part of healing, grounding and being present these days; I do this every single day of my life. I believe it's the same as praying or hypnosis; you need to have faith and hope in your heart to live in this world. I also go to sleep every night to an inner child healing meditation - even my husband accepts this as part of our bedtime routine! Ok, he doesn't like to admit to such airy-fairy healing stuff, but I know he secretly believes it and loves it too.

I practice Ho'oponopono, which is an ancient Hawaiian healing prayer. The power of this prayer is incredible, as are the many healing success stories that come with it. I hold so much belief and faith in this that I have I studied it and qualified to practice it. Morrnah was the original teacher to create a modern version of the Ho'oponopono that taught Dr Ihaleakala Hew Len PhD to practice and teach it. His story is incredible and a must-read.

A client's story

I had a client who had a whole lot of forgiveness to do. Her story amazed me. She had been with her then-husband since she was 15 years old, had been married for 29 years and had two children. She thought life was perfect as a stay at home mum, but as it turned out, it wasn't.

Her husband was holding onto something deep inside that was to eventually destroy the life she loved. He was a woman himself inside and this increasingly made a normal married life very difficult. She wanted, and continued to, for many years support her husband through this. However, over time she found it too unbearable to continue living a lie. She wanted her man back.

Eventually, none of them could live a lie any longer, so as you can imagine she had to go through a whole lot of grieving and emotional stress. Honestly, I don't think I have ever met a lady so considerate, understanding and thoughtful as her in all my life.

She was sad. She was holding on to blame, anger, sadness, resentment, you name it, and she had every right to feel these emotions. She was grieving. It brought major anxieties and a lot of self-doubt. She had to learn who she was and what she wanted for herself.

She felt guilty wanting to date again. She needed to feel wanted as a woman by a man again, learn to enjoy her own space and do whatever it took not to feel lonely. She had to let go of their friendship, which I have to say was beautiful, however, damaging at the same time, as having a constant reminder of what she craved and lost was causing more harm than good. So, you see sometimes we have to simply forgive to let go.

She had to learn to forgive herself and her ex. I was cheeky and told her she was more special than any other divorced women I had worked with as she was my only woman to marry a man and divorce a woman! Thankfully, she was able to share my humour in that.

Moving forward

> *"Why the hell should I forgive him for what he did to me and what he put me and my children through?"*

Yes indeed, good question, I thought. So, the obvious response was to get her to think about how she felt now. Who is in pain? Who is the one hurting here? And who is the only one suffering? She simply said, "well I am, of course".

Yes, you are, and do you think that you holding on to this anger and pointing the blame is going to solve anything or stop you feeling this way forever? The conversation and challenges continued and went much deeper for quite some time until she realised that she was the only one punishing herself, and to forgive would allow her the space in her head and the love for herself in her heart that she needed. This wasn't a quick fix; it took some work and tears, however, I'm pleased to say she does now forgive. Even if he is unaware of her forgiveness, she has allowed this for herself.

"I've tried to forgive, but it's not easy."

My response will always remain the same, "nope it's not!"

Anything worth working on will never be easy, however, it will be worth the investment in time and effort to get there.

Another client told me that I didn't know how it felt and I wouldn't forgive them if only I knew what he did to her. Ok, the truth is, at that stage she was right, I didn't know what he had done to her, just as she didn't know what I have had done to me. So, I said ok, you can either tell me and we'll compare notes, or you'll forget what the reason for forgiveness is and start forgiving anyway.

After all, forgiveness truly is an essential aid to recovery

Some tips and strategies to try for yourself at home

- ❖ Create yourself a forgiveness list including everyone you feel you need to forgive and another one with who you feel needs to forgive you.

- ❖ Think about who and how you have tried to forgive in the past and journal how this felt or any emotions that arise for you.

- ❖ Write a letter to your ex, getting all your feelings down, everything you wish you could have said to him - then read it to yourself and burn it. This is also great for releasing anger.

- ❖ Look up Morrnah's Prayer.

Ho'oponopono:

Please forgive me-I'm sorry-thankyou-I love you-I forgive myself

Detach to Attach

"We must be willing to let go of the life we planned so as to have the life that is waiting for us, follow your bliss and don't be afraid, and doors will open where you didn't know they were going to be."

"The cave you fear to enter holds the treasure you seek."

"People say that what we're all seeking is a meaning for life. I don't think that's what we're really seeking."

Joseph Campbell

At first letting go seems like the hardest thing you can do, yet once the reality of the why's and why not's hit you, everything will make sense and you'll be moving forward in no time.

I know we just covered a whole load on forgiveness, and you may at present believe they are one and the same, however, letting go and moving away from the past is a completely separate issue that needs addressing in a different way. Moving on involves detaching yourself from the past and attaching yourself to the future, hence the title of this chapter - detach to attach - your future; the future you're destined to have.

Reality check

You can't change the past - what's done is done, you've been there done that. What you do have to do is learn to accept what happened, regardless of any good or bad. None of that can change and really none of that matters in the bigger scheme of things.

You need to take that pressure off yourself. I mean seriously, do you need to plague yourself with any more crap than necessary? Why don't you try being nice to yourself for a change? Just think about the consequences that you'll live with if you don't do that now, think about how that will continue to lay heavy on you.

Holding on to emotions can make you store excessive weight. Yeah, I'm gutted about that one! Any undiagnosed physical aches and pains, you can bet your bottom dollar emotional baggage will be responsible for that one too. However, remind yourselves all this is temporary, you don't need to hold on to it forever, there is a cure.

Once you do stop holding on, you'll find you'll allow yourself to live a much healthier life and mind, especially when focusing head-on with the mental and emotional aspects.

Having the freedom and peace of mind to let go and fly away, it's true you'll feel free to live your life on your terms. I mean who doesn't want that? Clearing out the past, blowing off the cobwebs and making way for a new love or lover in your life. With the added bonus of letting go, you'll finally begin to feel worthy again. Surely that has to be worth effort and investment in yourself. Get yourself to the level of having great self-esteem and feel like you're in such a valuable place with yourself you could take on the world. If you don't follow your bliss or what actually brings you joy, someone else will just sweep along and do it for you.

Letting go

In my eyes, by not letting go you'll be in danger of staying stuck, just remaining the same as you are now, and stuck with the heavy burdens of the past and what it holds for you, being weighed down with all those mental and physical daily pains, dragging your enthusiasm and motivation down with it. Misery, bitterness and resentment shall continue to take over your heart, you'll destroy any chances of happiness, and lose out on so many opportunities waiting for you, including forming new relationships - platonic, family and loving ones – you'll just hang on to blame. Now that doesn't sound a very thrilling place to be to me - does it to you?

Look, I'm not saying any of this is easy, nor am I saying I did the right thing in the past. Let's face it, when my first husband and I had one conversation in the kitchen that almost led to immediate divorce, it made me feel at a loss; all I could do was think about my babies and all the promises of stability and security we had made for us and for them. I felt totally let down, unwanted, abandoned and rejected with no fight for us, nothing. So, in a state of panic, the first opportunity I got I met someone. Luckily, I fell in love with him and he was, to be fair, at the time a great stand-in. We later married and he was the father figure I wanted their natural father to be at the time, and he was the husband and family man I had always hoped for. Perfect until he decided to become a serial cheater. Back to square one it was for me.

You see, it's not always as simple as it looks, and I've learnt an awful lot since those days, thankfully. My point here is, don't rush straight from one disaster to another, take time out to process your feelings and emotions. Understand what you've been through, evaluate your options and think about where you're at before you even consider making huge life-changing decisions that can end up turning around and kicking you in the butt. For your own sanity, please do all that you can to get over the past or an ex before you move on to another, because let me tell you, this was only the starting point for me, I continued to jump in and out of relationships for the rest of my life until I hit rock bottom to face a reality check. I don't want that for any of you. I understand many of us need to get there first before we stand up and pay attention, however, if it can be avoided please act accordingly for your own benefits before you have to get to that horrific stage of your life.

Prepare yourself

Firstly, give yourself time, and I mean as long as it takes. That is of course as long as you're consciously making an effort to be kind to yourself in all areas of your life, and not by simply ignoring your feelings. Take the time to process your emotions and get to know your feelings. I highly recommend journaling these emotions and feelings for future reference.

Find your voice. I've never been quiet, but I know what it's like to not speak up when I could have, and by doing this we lose what we want. So, please take time to think for yourself and learn to speak out for yourself again. I know how difficult it is if you're an empath, or you've been in relationships where you were controlled or were a co-dependant and dare not even consider saying what was on your mind in the past, well this is your time now, so be brave and take small steps and test yourself on saying what the hell you really want.

Stand up with your head held high and become independent. After all, you really do need to start to make some decisions for yourself sometime soon, especially as I believe it's necessary to move forward from the old life you had. I promise you, the more you practice this the easier it gets, and you'll love making all your own decisions again. Just be sure you're thinking first and the decisions you're making are true to your heart and within your morals and ethics of the newer version of yourself.

Working at supporting yourself, for many of you beautiful souls out there, I know you never had to think about managing finances before, but this new empowered you will. Once you've gotten over the gremlins and hurdles, you will feel so independent and in control of yet another area of your life. Maybe this includes downsizing your home or car, or even taking on an extra shift or job, but do whatever it takes to bring in the income you need to gain your power to move forward alone.

Can you imagine how you're going to feel once you've found your voice and learned how to become independent? C.O.N.F.I.D.E.N.T. You're going to feel five inches taller (if you're a shorty like me, that's a good thing). You will feel amazing and liberated. After all, if you only have yourself to consider now, think about all the free time you'll have to do as you want, when you want and with whom you want. Now that in my eyes is worthy of detaching the past and attaching to a new you. Now darlings it's time to find your passion - have you ever had to think about what you want for yourself?

Treat this divorce or breakup you've been through as an open opportunity for a whole list of wonderful discoveries and adventures. Don't just sit there and think of it as a failure, how can it be a failure when you've learnt so many life skills during the marriage or relationship?

You've been given an opportunity to better yourself - either mentally, physically, socially or academically. The world is your oyster. Start from scratch and find out who you are again. Really take some time to get to know yourself; you'll be amazed how many of us didn't or don't know who we really are anymore. Think about it, you've had a life as a part of a unit, a husband or partner, which in turn brings his family and flaws, a house where I'm sure you did most of the household duties, the family - whether that's children or pets. You possibly had no time for just you, and maybe you lost yourself along the way, which could be absolutely fine, I'm not implying it's a bad thing if you were happy, but for many wives and mums we are very low in the pecking order of the care routine, right? Have a think about that person you became. Did you gain some nasty habits or flaws of your own you hadn't realised? You're likely to have made some mistakes along the way too. This is the time to check yourself out. As I said earlier, it's time for you now, you won't have to live under anyone else's rules or expectations, so don't waste valuable you time dwelling on the past and the what-ifs.

Welcome 'The Grey Rock Method'

I realised I've used this for so many years in the past, and then I discovered there was a name for it. It's truly a beneficial strategy to help you move and stop you from constantly going back or staying stuck in a place with someone who doesn't deserve you in their life, and especially for someone you deserve better than to have in your life. If you follow the guidelines, you'll be stepping away faster than you can say leap. In a nutshell, the grey rock method is simply a way of blanking out the ex, removing him from your existence. No more giving him the opportunity to pester you and give you doubts about not having him in your life anymore. Remember, you left for a reason, or he left you. Either way, you need to accept it isn't meant to be. Remove all access to you. Yes, that is right, do not allow him to know anything about where you are or what you're doing ever again.

Detach to Attach

Stop him in his tracks and take away all his power! Take away all of his control. Ouch, this one will hurt him the most!

Flat out ignoring him is the best action you could possibly do for yourself, and that means absolutely no contact - zilch-zero-none. This darling is the ultimate goal in detaching.

Yep, admittedly this is likely to be one of the hardest gifts you can give yourself, ever! But please remember, however hard this is at first, you'll soon reap the benefits and feel empowered.

Get back all he took from you, regain a fulfilled life and mind of your own again and allow yourself your own choices again. Without a shadow of a doubt, he's gonna use all of his charm and psychopathic ways to lure you back, batting his eyelashes or trying to buy your love back. But don't be fooled by this. I'm advising you now to keep your eyes wide open and look for the signs before you end up falling for it all over again.

He's not going to change into Prince Charming - you should know this by now.

By the way, ladies - don't be fooled, he knows exactly what buttons to press, he knows you remember. In fact, it's possible if he's a narcissist that he's created you, moulded you to be exactly how he needed you. He made you who you are so he can easily break you over and over and over!

You want to know how this is done?

It's as simple as putting him off you. You just need to be a bore who blends into the background and offer him no interest. Remember, make yourself undesirable to him.

- ❖ Get him to lose interest!
- ❖ Let him get bored with you.
- ❖ Deny him all access to you.
- ❖ Cut all ties.

This way he will tire of you because you're not feeding his cravings for drama. So, guess what - he's going to look elsewhere for his fix. How freaking awesome is that?

Delete his presence

The time has come to remove all those constant reminders - good and bad - happy or sad.

So, when you decide to make the move and remove all those photos of your ex - I'm not saying you have to burn them to the ground like some ritual (not that I'm against that either)!

Delete the photos, or put them on a CD, USB stick, or whatever technical device you know about that I don't! Then bury them in the attic, loft or basement - or maybe return to sender? That sounds fun, hey! If you share children, maybe make a beautiful keepsake (after all you are both their parents and they would be delighted when they're older) and store them away for them at a much later date. But for now, remove them out of your sight.

All those pet names- darling, babe, love of my life, soulmate, sperm donor, hubby poos (yep done that one too), that you have stored - change to their given name. Trust me it's worth it if someone sees your messages or calls come up - keep it clean and civil. Do not have family framed pictures up all over your house - stash them for the kids later. You don't need to have a Greek dinner smash down dance now do you?

Social media - wow now here's a job. Change the nickname in Messenger, remove your married status and life events that you'll be seeing in memory hop - have a good clear out. It's amazing to have that relief and that breath of fresh air feeling afterwards. Don't forget the others like Instagram, Snapchat Viber, WhatsApp, Twitter and LinkedIn. Get rid of them. You don't need to see what they had for lunch or where they visited - no stalking required - remove him from them all, you don't need to know, and you don't need him to know your business either. Another tip some of you may find useful, especially if you've left a narcissistic relationship - remove their friends and family too – so they have limited ways to stalk and hunt you.

Knowing all this will create space for new thoughts and emotions - a happier environment to look forward and by removing this part of your past you will prevent lasting emotions of anger- sadness- fear- pain and long-term disappointment.

What to do now

"How am I supposed to move on from him when I have so many reminders everywhere I turn?"

The answer is above - delete him and remove all existence of him from your life.

"I'll never be able to forget him, he was the love of my life."

Yep aren't they all, however, letting go and moving on doesn't mean you have to completely forget them, it simply means allowing what was, be, and not allowing past memories - good or bad - control your future.

"What am I supposed to do to move on"?

Firstly, accept that you can't change any past events, anything that was done, or pain caused to you. Next is to understand that detaching yourself from the pain doesn't mean you're entirely moving on, just attaching yourself to your own future.

Some tips and strategies

❖ Take the time you need, there is no rush, however, don't use this as an excuse to hold on as an escape to moving on, be kind to yourself.

❖ Try my Top 10 Tips for letting go http://bit.ly/35YYlvx

Reconnect with Self

Repeat of a truth - you are never going to be who you once were! She's already gone. You need to get used to the fact that you've already changed and learn who the new you is, or at least who you can become.

Zelda Marsh

You are likely to be the most precious best friend you'll ever have in your life.

I mean let's face it, you're stuck with each other forever. I say each other because as you may be well aware, you have a conscious self and a subconscious self and more often than not your egotistical self (conscious) rules over the inner self (subconscious). So, doesn't it make sense to treat her with the respect, kindness, appreciation and love she so does deserve? Try and treat her in a way you'd want others to treat you and you may just wake up and be surprised to witness this amazing act of attitude become a reality.

No one knows you like you, in fact I'd go to say a lot of you don't even know who you are yourselves anymore, and that's a scary thought isn't it? I mean, if you don't know who you really are then how can you expect others to know who you are, what you like or dislike? And even more to the point, how can anyone else possibly love you for you, or love you your way, if you don't even know what your way is?

Who are you anymore?

I have to admit, as much as this sounds amazing and obvious to many, I found this the most difficult part to grasp, all my life thinking I loved everyone and myself equally. How wrong I was.

Going through all the challenges and life-changing situations that being divorced can bring you will certainly force you unknowingly to push yourself way down the pecking order of priorities when it comes to self-care or self-worth, and it's highly likely that you'll lose sight of who you really are by now.

You absolutely do deserve to work out what it is that you've lost inside. I can tell you that, for many of us, divorce not only changes everything in our lives, it changes the woman we knew. So, think strong and hard about that one, as now you need to accept that you'll never be "yourself" again because that girl has gone. She's done and dusted. Now what we have in front of us is a fine figure of a life-experienced, powerful woman of the world waiting to bounce back and reclaim herself.

You've heard the expression "finding yourself" many times, and I know it sounds cliché but it's true and that's exactly what you need to do - find out who you are, look for the changes. They won't all be good but they are part of you and you need to learn to accept and love all parts of who you have become. No holding back, no hiding, just loving all of your flaws and quirks. Oh, it's not easy by the way, but do be prepared to feel abso-freaking-lutely amazing when you do get there!

The limits of how amazing are endless and priceless. You'll be filled to the brim with confidence, and by that I mean a non-fake, put on a facemask kind of confidence. You'll have a bounce in your step again, or maybe you'll discover a bounce for the first time in your life. Can you remember the last time you felt that great?

Imagine waking up feeling total gratification for every single thing in your existence, such as waking up after an awesome night's sleep, waking up to no alarm even - I love that one - listening to the birds or the weather outside, stepping outside and breathing in, smelling the morning air and holding gratitude for that just in itself. Loving the sound of your children or pets fussing around, smiling as you prepare your breakfast, enjoying preparing for the day ahead.

Gratitude and possibilities

Listening to a podcast or a favourite tune, reading a few pages from a new book, how about loving the outfit you decide to wear today, enjoying a class that will stretch your body, and not always to its limits I may add!

You'll discover that you're at a stage where everything in your world will just flow. Whatever is going on around you, just imagine having a place to take in and appreciate what exists. And finding that time in your life again when you'll get the urge to do more and more every single day. And for a minute sit yourself in a quiet place with no distractions and imagine when smiling every day becomes natural.

The trouble you'll continue to have if you have no desire to reconnect with yourself is that you're in danger of staying and feeling exactly as you do now and I know how that can't be an option for so many of you lovely ladies out there, it just can't.

Please don't tell me that you're happy living in the shadows of your better self, that part of you that enjoys living in the past, wanting to hang on to your youth or the naïve prospect of returning to that woman you were all those years ago - **NOPE!** Forget it, give yourself a big fat shake and get real darlings, that day has gone, you're going to end up feeling empty and lost.

I assure you, living a life with low self-esteem ain't pretty. You can sugar-coat it all you like and go back to the blame game, however, you're responsible for how you feel in the bigger scheme of things. So, believe me when I say living with no confidence and low self-esteem is not a place you wanna reside for long.

How can you go on with your life without feeling any true value to yourself? You can't possibly give true value or love to others when you don't hold genuine love and value for yourself. Jeez, I feel like a stuck record now, but I'm so passionate about getting this message to each and every one of you out there. Divorce and breakups kill a part of your soul - so go and grab it back - find something deep inside yourself and raise that goddess that exists inside of you all and bounce the frig back into life, don't remain a co-dependant all your lives.

I found it hard

Learning to love myself had to have been the most traumatic part of my healing process. That may sound a bit extreme, but it's true. I had invested in a few programs with mentors and coaches - both spiritual - yet covered different areas, so between them a whole

Reconnect with Self

lot of work was involved, including meditating, healing, praying, diagnosing who I was and what my life had consisted of, as well as relationships with money, my past and myself. That is just a brief outline; the work was full-on and consistent.

When I was first asked to take part in an inner child meditation (which I hadn't heard of back then), I was an emotional wreck, in front of a room full of others in a similar situation, of course. Believe it or not, after that experience I felt compelled to commit to a year-long program. Then I rejected the inner child part for quite some time, which is what we do. I recall very vividly doing all sorts of different activities at a retreat, and one involved doing deep inner child meditation work, in fact it was three different versions of it.

The first I sailed through, as I was now used to it and comfortable reaching to my inner child, the second involved bringing our parents in, which I was ok with yet very surprised by my findings and reactions, however it made perfect sense to me in the end, and I have to say opened my eyes and changed my relationship with them, or at least my dad from then on in. The third stage was bringing in our abusers, well there was no way I could do that, so I laid there with my eyes open, all the way through it, I just couldn't bring myself to go there. My spiritual teacher and mentor spotted me and indicated I close my eyes - I could not, so at the end of this particular session I was asked to discuss how I felt. I just said blatantly I didn't want to, so then I felt like a naughty schoolgirl which followed with the facts on repressing and storing said emotions, which then brought me into another emotional meltdown. I felt like I had months on an emotional rollercoaster from here on in.

Also, I had invested in a lightworkers business coaching program with two beautiful souls. Their aim was to bring lightworkers to get paid their worth and also find their niche in their required business modality. This was a major contributor to the emotional rollercoaster as one of the first parts of this program included the hero's journey. This was the hardest part for me, as to discover your life's purpose or niche, you start by writing the first half of your life down. For me that was the first 25 years of my life down, ok I was stuck already, I didn't have much to go on at this stage. I asked my mum for a few ideas of the early years then had to have healing sessions and extra meditations to bring back some of my pigeonholed memories. Ok, now I had realised why they were pigeonholed, I didn't want to relive some of these memories at all.

I even got to one stage where I wanted to believe some of them were made up in my subconscious bank (as I call it). Anyway, they weren't, as I went on to discover as the layers were unfolding more and more of these memories surfaced. Then came the second 25 years and I had some pretty beautiful memories amongst some graphic ones towards the end. However, damage was done for me, I had to deal with all of this shit that I didn't want to. I had to take time out and think about how I felt now, and how I was going to move forward with all these memories. So, you can imagine these two had their work cut out for them. I had a whole lot of healing sessions thrown in to get me through this- thankfully they really were amazing. Other parts of this work involved the realisation that I didn't hold any love for myself, I mean I've always been loving so I couldn't work out what was meant by that.

I soon did. I was introduced to Louise Hay's mirror work. Now, don't get me wrong, I was aware of Louise Hay yet hadn't come across her mirror work before, and as a woman, of course I knew how to look in a mirror as it was my daily occurrence. **Holy shit**, no one could have prepared me for the shock on how humiliated and weird I felt having to look in a mirror and tell myself I love you! I mean, who the hell does that? I'm not ugly but I didn't put myself out there as vain either, this was how little I thought of me and the love I held for myself?

Reconnect with Self

How shallow does that make me sound? All the times I used to judge others for admiring themselves in windows or mirrors in the past, it was because I never felt it or understood the reality behind self-love, I had none.

I now introduce this powerful technique to all my clients, and it is interesting to learn that I'm not alone in the discomfort with this. I do feel fortunate, however, to know that I was self-loving in lots of other areas that helped me no end, unlike many of my clients who have no idea, and that is sad to learn.

Other work included a whole lot of daily journaling, and this is when I decided to take a Diploma in Journal Therapy. I would highly recommend using this for any form of healing and yes, I do use this still - hence the book!

I was reading and listening to as many self-love books, quotes, movies and meditations as I could possibly fit in - you could say I overdosed myself in love. This time it was self-love. Let's face it, I had almost 50 years to catch up on, so it wasn't going to happen overnight at any normal pace.

One of the amazing books I listened to (audiobooks are amazing for a busy woman), was Embrace Yourself by Taryn Brumfitt. She is my type of girl; down-to-earth and a real woman with real expectations and views of the woman's body. She made me feel ok being me, ok with my flaws, ok with my lumps and bumps. I am so good at giving praise and compliments to any other woman in the world but struggled when it came to me. I have always been my own worst critic, and nothing had ever been good enough on me, for me or to me! I learnt that's normal when you don't love yourself properly. So, I highly recommend this to every woman.

The next steps

One of the self-love acts that I had got right since departing my monster, was to learn parts of who I was, what I liked and how to enjoy being on my own, and that included spending time by myself alone and being more than ok with that. Oh, don't get me wrong, this was new to me - I had a life hating my own space, dreaded being on my own, I mean I had a young life of responsibilities and siblings, then started my own family at 20, to being a child/adult / wife/partner/mum/colleague/boss/friend. You name it, I always had a role to play and it generally involved doing for others.

So, when I got to the point of having to flee my hometown, my career, my family and my friends (which were my life), after I had gone through my OCD meltdown, Cinderella stage, I decided I needed to busy myself and try to resume a normal life, earning money and living independently again. As I mentioned previously, I got a job as a live-in personal assistant for spinal injured individuals. This way I had work, company, money (I owed so many people back for giving me handouts as I had nothing) and this meant I didn't have to think about putting some permanent roots down and decide where I could live. I talk about this some more in the monster chapter.

Taking the job brought me so much free time. As you can imagine, some of the individuals I worked with didn't go far and I was basically on standby to fit into their lives. I met some incredible individuals and visited some amazing new places. Until eventually I got my permanent client. I felt at home there; he and his family were close and they were so inviting. I loved it, we were always involved in activities and we got on really well. In fact, after a while we often acted like a married couple, bickering and complaining to each other. It was a real shame to leave him, which I only did to start my new life in Australia. He did introduce me to Costa Coffee at the Cheddar Gorge, which became my favourite spot in Somerset.

Reconnect with Self

While I had all these spare hours and days, I was introduced to Netflix, reading, and lots of other towns and cities I hadn't even heard of before. I felt alive. I dated myself on days off, like going for a slap-up meal in a lovely restaurant in Plymouth on the harbour with a glass of wine and a seafood platter. This was a luxurious treat and I loved it. I got myself a statement tattoo, I went to a safari and laughed at the monkeys destroying David (my car). I found life and fun on my own. So, you see I had started back then this journey of self-discovery and self-love.

I urge you to see how possible it is to love yourself eventually and how life can become the life you deserve to live once you put some love, time and investment into yourself, show yourself how much you really are worth it, show yourself how you need to feel.

What to do now

A lady recently complained that it was different for her because she was no 'oil painting'. Yes, I know how she felt and the past version of me would just feel that as a trigger and want to hug her. She still gets the hug, however, I do get so upset hearing this come out of the mouth of any woman. In my opinion this is used as an excuse not to love themselves. I told her she was perfectly beautiful exactly how she was; she wasn't meant to be any other way. I sent her off with a list of daily affirmations and told her to repeat all day long until she finally started to believe herself, because if she didn't believe it, how on earth was anyone else going to think she was beautiful? Our minds are clever and devious bastards at times, and they will believe whatever we put in .

This was me to a tee, I had in my head as I was informed by a client one day, "I've always loved helping other people more, because I'm a caring giving person". "Yes," I respond, "I've lived this role all my life so I can compassionately add that I know how and why you feel this way, and yes it feels good to help, but you're actually neglecting yourself, you're putting yourself at the bottom of the pecking order, meaning, you're putting less value on yourself. You can love and care for others far greater when you show yourself the love and kindness you deserve." Like I said earlier, if you don't love yourself, how can others love you?

Another wonderful question that came my way was, "how can I reconnect with myself?" I love this, and many of us women, especially after a trauma much like a divorce and facing so many challenges will have lost sight of themselves, so what I suggest is that you start from the very basics of getting to know yourselves and what makes you tick, what brings you joy and then once you get that part nailed, you can then move on to other areas of yourself and eventually truly embrace the authentic, beautiful you.

Reconnect with Self

Some of the tricks or strategies

❖ Do the Louise Hay mirror work. Get a hand mirror and talk sense to yourself, tell you how ok you are then move on to the love you part. Look her up and watch how she talks about doing this; Louise really makes it look easy.

❖ Learn to embrace yourself - love your curves and how your skin feels, jump up and down and watch the wobbles wobble if you have any extra padding! Play with your hair and enjoy each strand. Count your greys if you have any. Look deeply into your eyes, see all those unique flecks and shapes that only you have. Make yourself laugh out loud, even if you're the only one who knows what you're laughing at. Have a dress up day - this could be a diva or a clown; have fun with you.

❖ Go on a date with yourself - book a beautiful meal in a lovely restaurant (tell them it's for one, that way there should be only one place setting, you don't want to sit there looking like you've been stood up). Get yourself all dolled up, hair nails and face on. Don't knock it, how many times have you gone all out, no expense spared to date a man? Are you saying you're not worth it? I hope not, because you are. Now go and prove it.

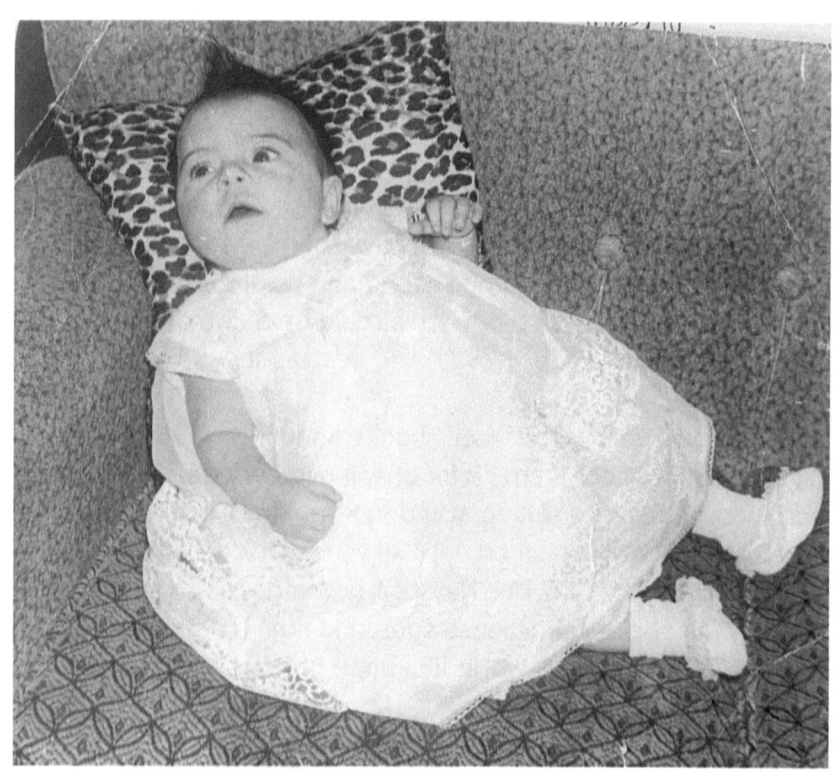

Passion and Purpose

"The beauty of a woman is not in a facial mode but the true beauty in a woman is reflected in her soul. It is the caring that she lovingly gives, the passion that she shows, the beauty of a woman grows with the passing years."
Audrey Hepburn

"To aim high will get you closer to something - to not aim at all will get you nowhere."
Zelda Marsh

Knowing what you want out of life isn't as easy as you may think.

Our passions most certainly change as life goes on. Well they should do anyway. Or maybe, just maybe, you are one of those few and fortunate enough to know exactly what your life's purpose is and you already know exactly what you have in store for your future and everything you desire in life. If so, this chapter may not be for you.

For the rest of us, life's not always that plain sailing is it? For many of us life has a way of getting to us and creating obstacles for what we would ideally love our lives to look like, and quite often our motivation is nothing like we need it to be and without a big ass shove in the right direction that goes down the pan too.

Do you know what motivates you? I know my motivation levels have altered a lot over my years. Schooling was always my first form of motivation and safe go-to as a child, away from home anyway, so I strived to succeed, I wanted to be good, I wanted to feel that someone was proud of me, so I studied and excelled wherever I could. I carried this on into my adulthood; whenever something was failing in an area of my life, I buried the painful parts and took up the space in my brain, and filled it with knowledge, then it was always my children, then it was my men, or the men should I say! Then it became my job, now it's living and helping the right people.

Passion

My love for love, food and health have always played a massive motivation for me. This doesn't mean I've always had this great urge to wake up with a massive surge of passion and motivation for my day, however, that was my thing, I didn't know anything else, I didn't know how to aspire to anything, or feel passionate about opportunities and self-development, I only knew how to love others, because I was searching and I'd like to think I did that very well.

I always found myself loving to help others, having this amazing ability to see deep inside of people. Maybe I'm a soul-seeker, however, I can usually find the best version of people, and knowing I could help them find themselves, or see the best in themselves then make them feel fabulous and non-judged, made me a great friend/colleague/teacher and partner.

This came at a price as being this person made me forget and most often neglect my own needs, wants and at many points in life passions, let alone have any other thoughts on my purpose. Maybe I was already living it, maybe that's all I was supposed to be here for - to care for and serve others.

I'm not alone, it's not just me though.

The fact that we were all born with a life's purpose and that we quickly begin to lose sight of this and the knowledge of what that purpose is as soon as we became aware of our surroundings as a child, then all that our environment gives us, it then in turn takes all of our abilities to search for or at least remember our purpose. For many of us it then it takes us our entire lifetime - or so it feels for many of us - searching and searching to find it again.

My Purpose

Purpose is supposed to be your guide for life decisions as it influences our behaviour. Then in this case I guess I had lived the purpose I was meant to, for at the time I did with the knowledge I had, and I can accept that now. Doing this I know is not entirely true, I now know that I have developed so many life skills and lessons from the life I have been given.

My purpose, although it remains to care for and serve, has developed to a much deeper and meaningful service. I will always love no matter what, I know this with all my heart and soul. I will always use my knowledge as a teaching method to serve others, however, this time my purpose will include loving myself with the passion I should, and to use this passion to help so many other women and serve with them to be the women they are meant to be, to overcome any life trauma caused by others, especially after divorce and all that comes with it.

I know my love and compassion will serve great justice to the world and the universe. I will teach so many women with my passion to overcome abuse and trauma and not allow anyone else's actions get in the way of the life we want to live; the life in fact we are destined to live. As I love to say, "we can bounce that passion back into our lives and reclaim that purpose, what is rightfully ours".

And once you do discover what your purpose is, you'll find the true reason to live, have those butterflies going crazy again, without the aid of a man! How amazing does the prospect of having something to look forward to on a daily basis feel like to you? Just reflect on that for a moment. That would be an amazing achievement for anyone who's lost that feeling or even worse lost everything else in life before today. And for any women who have been through a divorce or two, you'll know all about loss, on so many angles, I'm sure.

All is not lost, you shall see! I want you to be reassured and know that you truly can feel happiness again, and you can find whatever it is that fulfils you again, or if not again, for the first time. All this is in your power, it's in your reach, you're designed to have purpose.

Dreams

Do you really think dreams are made up? If so, by who and who puts them in our minds? Do you believe they're just a fantasy or a figment of our imaginations? Well some of them may well be, however, to me dreams are a reality; they are placed in our minds and imagination for a reason, a purpose - our purpose - you can't make this shit up! How many times have you had crazy dreams and ignored them? I dare you to sit back and journal as many of those dreams as you can, then go through them, have them analysed too. Not all dreams are as you believe them to be, even a so-called nightmare isn't all you believe. Whatever goes on in your subconscious is a reflection of your conscious self. Conscious or egotistical dreams can also be achieved, the power of belief is amazing, and if you do set goals to accomplish your desires, at least you'll strive to get something closer than you would have if you do nothing.

Remember, if you do nothing, nothing will change!

Stay as you are, do you?

Think this is bringing you happiness? Obviously not, otherwise you wouldn't be attracted to reading this right now. You must be seeking something.

If you decide to do nothing, then at least you know you're responsible for never discovering and unveiling your true purpose or feeling, that inner passion. Please don't let the fire deep inside your soul fizzle away. You have so much to give, it hurts me that so many of us are not motivated or giving ourselves the chance. We deserve to feel alive and kicking. Maybe it takes losing a life the kick up the ass attitude to want to have one? I have to admit nearly not having one did that for me, and I hold daily gratitude I'm here today doing all I do - living and loving my life that I still have.

Could you bear the fact that doing nothing could leave you living a life of what-ifs and regrets? Why wait until you're on your death bed and say to yourself or loved ones "if only" or, "I wish I'd done this or that"? You have this perfect opportunity to at least try, unless of course you like wasting this amazing life you were given and would rather be bored, as doing nothing will get it setting in rather quickly, or depression will soon creep up on you and kick in, leaving you with no hope in front of you!

Taking risks and discoveries

In October 2016 I took one of the biggest risks of my life and left England for a life in Australia. I had no idea if this would work out well long term or not when I made the decision to go. I do know that I couldn't live in the shadows of fear and misery that I had for long enough. Something had to give, so what was I to lose, you may ask? Ok my home, my family, my friends, my entire life as I knew it.

Have I ever looked back? HELL NO!

Ok, so I had met Geoff (you'll learn more later in the book) and we had travelled around Queensland for around three months, stayed in my daughter's shed! I know how that sounds, but that's what we call it. Living here and having far too much time on my hands, one day Geoff asked me what I liked doing; what were my interests, hobbies and what do I do. So, like I told him, I love anything, I'm happy doing anything and everything. This caused frustration because he didn't get an answer. In reality I didn't have one, *I had no freaking idea what I liked to do* - how could I, I'd been a mum, a wife, a partner, a carer, a boss, you name it I was everything but a *me*!

Don't get me wrong, I absolutely do take great joy in so many experiences and adventures - I love reading, participating and doing! Anything. However, this was a gigantic turning point for

Passion and Purpose

me, because I knew there and then I needed to know, I needed find my passion, I wanted my purpose, the one that was meant for me now, and this was when my journey of self-discovery took a massive step, well a few massive steps as it happens.

As I was developing in all areas of my life, I had taken a few steps in various directions that led me to going back into business on my own, using all the holistic therapies I had achieved years ago, and had let them go dormant while working in another field.

I decided to start with massage therapies and this has become quite successful, however, as I'm getting older, this became a strain on my body, especially as I discovered the pains were due to osteoarthritis, I felt I needed to change direction or at least follow my intuition, so I started meditating all day, every day. I moved on to studying and qualifying with diplomas in crystal healing therapy, reiki, intuitive tarotology, ancient Egyptian magic, journal therapy, then spiritual life coaching. Yes, as you learned earlier, I do bury my head in studies and have developed the will to gain extra knowledge.

Being the type of person I am, I could not go out and work in an area I haven't experienced myself, so I invested in a life coaching program or two of my own. In doing this I was subjected to a whole lot of trauma and mind-blowing discoveries about myself and my past; the past I had buried so deep I had forgotten existed or at least wasn't even sure if they were even real memories or some make-believe figment of my imagination.

So yes, as traumatic as it was, at least I had discovered who I was, why I became the woman I had and suddenly my life purpose was unveiled. My life found a passion again. **I knew what I had to do and where I had to go from there.**

Deep and meaningful

I don't know how many of you have ever had to discuss or even attempt to unveil every single year of your life, including each significant or momentous occasion for each year of your life before. Well, if you have then you'll understand to some degree how difficult this can be. If you haven't, I urge you to do it - maybe under the guidance of a support system, like a coach or a therapist; this is not a place of self-discovery to be had alone. I certainly wouldn't haven't managed this alone; I had no idea at first what this was going to achieve. So hard work, tears and tantrums later, it was to unveil the patterns I had formed in my life and why. Woah! What a revelation this turned out to be, what a shocker! It's an interesting concept and an incredible experience listening to someone peel back the layers of your life and disclose your patterns and, in turn, purpose.

Hero's journey, yes it has a name and it's created or at least became well known by the famous Joseph Campbell. He explains how you can see from all of your life's events how you become the person you are today, and with this how you can begin to serve your purpose. So, knowing that we had unveiled all of my life history with my coaches, which by the way, oh, how I love those two for all the effort, hours and dedication they shared as we went through this massive journey together, knowing all my secrets. And then came the point of choosing my purpose, or my niche as it was. Yes, another battle and this took some time to get my head around, however, it all made perfect sense in the end. Until the unveil was to become public. WHAT THE ACTUAL FUCK! I'd spent my entire life hiding and pigeon-holing all this shit, to be told that the only way to heal and work closely with the women in the world of my niche was to openly share my experiences, and my life story.

Yeah right! Now I went back to a childlike spoilt brat attitude and dug my heels right in. I was a rebel, there was no freaking way on

Passion and Purpose

this actual earth I was telling anyone any of that crap. Anyway, who wants to hear about the sick or unhealthy experiences I had gone through, who cares? Why should I?

To wean me in gently (ha, so they say), I was to start to talk about my authentic self in the safe environment of the closed group my coaches provided us with. So, I would add a few stories here and there, and yes, I was getting braver at sharing, until I got the bang on the head and was asked to do a live video to our group! You'd think a loud-mouth, opinionated me would breeze through this, wouldn't you? Well I kid you not, I was a dithering wreck.

I can't even remember what I actually spoke about, but I do remember crying and shaking for around two hours afterwards. What was wrong with me? I used to be able to get up in front of 20 to 30 of my care staff and run meetings without a flaw or a wince. Yet talking about me and my stuff was a different kettle of fish entirely. I couldn't do it, I wasn't doing that. Ok, I did continue to do that, and it got easier, then came to the public revelation - nothing could prepare me for this, I was crying and screaming at my husband about how incompetent I must be, because I couldn't get the balls to talk on a video to myself. It's not like anyone else had to be around - talk about ridiculous - and way out of my comfort zone.

He reassured me and even suggested I pretend I was talking to him (that didn't work), however something inside me knew I had to share my version of life, my journey, my survival, my BounceBackAbility with all these women to inspire them and give them the hope to continue with life and find it inside themselves to live the life they deserve to live; happy and confident within themselves. As with everything else, I got there.

You see, finding your purpose and passion may well not be easy, however, it will be worth it, and you can do it. Be strong, be brave, be persistent, be positive and be supported. Now I have my own demons to share and proof of how it can affect us all. When asked by a previous client, "how do I discover my life's purpose and passion?" I could just relay my version of how I found mine and allow hers to come to light.

What to do now

Again, I came across a wonderful yet somewhat mature lady who had divorced from her previous husband after 34 years together. She had no idea who she was anymore, understandably. She had been a mum and a wife all her life until that point. So, she wanted to know what she liked and how she could learn new activities in her "old age". In her case we simply went down to the basics and started small. We set some very simple tasks and goals, a lot of journaling and unveiling. I think she was surprised to find out how well she remembered some of the old tricks she had up her sleeve from back in the day.

I think my most challenging client was desperately keen to hold on to how she was, she didn't want to change, she wanted to feel bitter and have no hope, this way her ex-husband would feel guilty for her pain. It took a lot of work to get through to her and allow her to realise she was only punishing herself at the end of the day and she wouldn't ever find happiness if she didn't do anything positive or make any changes. I'm happy to say she has now made some positive changes and no longer punishes herself or her ex, however, she is still a work in progress.

Making changes has to be a priority when moving on in the direction you need to. It is vital that you remember you will not, and can't ever, remain the woman you once were. It's impossible, so don't waste your time trying to recreate her. Instead, bounce your little self back up and reclaim your life; the new life that you deserve to live.

Why don't you have a bit of self-discovery right now? Get a book and a pen and start writing everything you are grateful for. Expand your mind and remember it's often the simplest of things that bring you joy and gratitude. You may even surprise yourself. This is an awesome step into knowing what you do and don't like.

Here is a list of 10 steps you can take to find your passion and purpose.

- What are your two best qualities?
- Create a life's purpose statement.
- Explore the things you love or would love to do.
- Reflect on your happy moments.
- Write down all the moments you've felt fulfilled.
- Follow your intuition/heart/gut feelings and what it is telling you.
- Make sure your purpose and passions are in alignment with your skills and experiences.
- Be clear about what your purpose is, think about what excites you as you reflect on this.
- Write down x 15 times, (like lines at school) "My life is perfect when…"
- I dare you to live your life as if you are already living your life purpose with passion.

Answer these goal-setting questions, then feel free to add a bunch of your own:

- Am I where I want to be right now?
- Have I accomplished all I thought I would have by now?
- Am I enjoying my lifestyle, my diet, my job, my friends, my leisure/play time -do I feel rewarded?
- Am I fulfilled in my career or business?
- Could my relationships be any more meaningful?

Now you've set yourself up on a journey of goal setting and life searching, what shall you do next, I wonder?

Discovering your Tribe

"Don't expect your friend to be a perfect person, but help your friend become a perfect person, that's true friendship."

Mother Teresa.

"Real friends are like diamonds, bright, beautiful, valuable and always in style."

Nicole Richie.

Fact-study shows that it takes an average of 50 hours to consider someone new as a casual friend, 90 hours to be classed as a real friend and a whole 200 hours of time to become a close friend.

Journal of social and personal relationships.

A best friend is like having a therapist and a sister rolled into one for life.

A true friend is someone who lets you have total freedom to be yourself - now who doesn't want that in their life?

First of friends

I recall my very first best friend; I was 17 years old and working in a fresh fish factory in the gruesome town of Grimsby.

Our first meeting was on a process line in the fish factory. Two teenage girls without a care in the world, working in a cold, wet, smelly factory, just trying to earn enough money to live as neither of us had aspirations for much more at the time.

Stuck in this hell-hole of a place, I recall her asking me my name and with my response she burst into a full-on belly laugh, which in turn made me laugh. We both got into trouble for laughing and not working as we should have been. That was the moment we became friends and we've remained friends ever since. In fact, I still to this day hold her close in my heart and consider her my oldest friend (not just in age I may add), known as my Queen, my rock and my roll. We have shared so many wonderful and tragic memories - we had children around the same time, we had mutual friends who had children at the same time, we divorced around the same time the first time around too - amazing isn't it? And we have both created amazing lives for ourselves, so we should be very proud of how we have progressed from the smelly, laughing days of mischievousness.

My queen was to become the one person to link me to my future - I mean what are the odds that one woman would accidentally introduce you to the man you'd marry - thrice (that's three separate men/husbands)! You couldn't put bets on that happening, could you? She was to become the woman that I shared most of my life events with- we even had connections with the monster.

Making friends

Being the kind of gal who moved from home to home, town to town and man to man, I had never really had time to make friends very often. Don't get me wrong, living that life made me resilient, and I'd find it easier to just get to know many people I stumbled across, but not get close.

As life progressed and I built my own tribe, I found a few I could trust my life with. I haven't seen any of them for years, however, I know hand on heart if I needed them, they'd show up without any question, as I know if they needed me, I'd be there too.

That's my girls - my tribe - my loves from England.

Each and every one of these ladies have served a place and a purpose in my life. Some have been even lifesaving. You know who you are darlings and you know I love you. One particular woman who is better known as my soul mate was to become a huge part in my life. I couldn't believe a woman that chose me in the Yellow Pages, would become a friend, one of my staff and my soul mate; we had so many identifiable traits.

True value of your tribe

The value of having a tribe or go-to for support, sharing, laughter and love is absolutely vital and paramount to survive as a woman in this world.

"Men are from Mars and women are from Venus." Women are different to men. We think differently, we act completely separately, we problem solve oppositely, (trust me you know what I mean by this). Us women multi-task whereas men and actually some women only view in black and white, which can be bloody frustrating.

Men are not emotionally driven like us women; men are logically driven. Yes, I know this is hard to comprehend at times but it's scientifically proven. I mean, I've been proud of the fact that I've been logically-minded and an outside the box thinker, but science is science so I shall just take their word for it! My point here being that men and women are different, and as much as we often need each other to create a balance, women need women friends and that's all there is to it!

We need each other.

Did you know that women with early stage breast cancer were four times more likely to die if they didn't have any friends than those who did?[3] – Wow, now to me that really is the power of the tribes.

You can see why we need to be upping our contact time and creating new bonds, or at least decide where they shall fit.

We are strong characters when it comes to girl power, we bond and we seem to have this amazing ability to talk to each other for hours and hours on end about our problems, issues, thoughts, feelings, triumphs and tribulations, even sex. We listen to each other and share stories equally. Even when we disagree on something, we get over it and move on quickly.

We laugh, we cry, we assist each other through a trauma or a crisis, we bring each other up when we're down, even when you're going through the toughest time yourself, you know your girlfriend is

---

[3] Breastcancer.org research the journal of cancer 2012

getting her support and your shoulder first, that's us , that's friends, that's our tribe, us girls make it work.

Just to go on about how amazing having your tribe is a little longer, think about this for a minute:

- ❖ When you're feeling pants or a bit down and you need a pick-me-up, who you gonna call? And the answer is not ghostbusters, it's your girl.

- ❖ When you're sad and you need a shoulder to cry on without judgement, who you gonna call?

- ❖ You're in need of a break, you know she's there.

- ❖ Your man or your family just don't get you or how you're feeling, where are you getting your emotional support from? Yes again, there she is.

- ❖ Who knows your deepest darkest secrets and still loves you? Unconditionally too.

- ❖ I mean, who else would get away with telling you your outfit looks shocking, your hair's a mess, or the man you're dating is a douchebag?

Yep, your girls have your back. Whether you listen to them or not, they will be brutally honest with you and you'll still love their souls. With your besties you'll always have a sex therapist and a shopping buddy thrown in too.

New tribes

Don't tell me finding your tribe isn't important wherever you are or whatever you're going through.

If you are divorced and you've had to lose your tribe because they can't move with you, or they've moved on with their lives (this happens to us all) or they sided with him, refresh and find a new tribe.

When you have found your new friend or tribe, you'll again have someone to share your stories with. You'll discover a whole new perspective on your life as it was and is; how much fun can that be? You'll never get lonely with new buddies. Just think, brand new friends not only open you up to millions of new opportunities, you get new contacts, new hobbies and interests thrown in; this new life of yours will become so freaking amazing, why are you holding on to the friends you don't have anymore?

Let go and discover what new people in your life have to offer you.

Open your imagination and eyes to the new interests and adventures that can come your way. Think about this new life you're creating and all this amazing self-esteem you're going to gain. All these new or old friends will keep you happier longer, so with happiness we create health. So, friends equal a happier, healthier life, who doesn't want that?

A life without friends is a lonely and dark place to be. I'm not saying you need more than one to survive, I'm saying you need at least one woman to trust and rely on for each other. Don't think you're being selfish wanting to offload on your girls; that's what we're here for.

Don't feel guilty needing time to share. Look, we all need alone time, but as social creatures we need people around us too, and there is someone for everyone, you don't need to isolate yourself because you're timid and daren't speak to the new neighbours; find another way to attract your own sort. Don't sit at home being miserable and allowing yourself to fall into depression, there will be another girl out there feeling exactly like you; be there together.

As you can see, it is valuable and precious to have good friends around. I'm not saying the friends you already have or the ones you may lose are totally replaceable, but you do need to increase your tribe to suit your lifestyle and location.

If you really do struggle making friends, at least get a support system from somewhere.

You've just read all the reasons we need friends or support and I know there will be a million other reasons that are unique to you.

Changes

I moved to the other side of the world where I knew three adults in the entire country of Australia, and that's one of the largest countries in the world. Do you think I only know those three adults now? Most certainly not. Through work, places I've lived and my businesses I have created a huge tribe again, only this time my friends, colleagues, acquaintances and clients are all different and all serve a very different purpose in my life. We are all there for each other and my social life is as full or quiet as I choose these days.

I don't want to hear excuses of how many of you are now living miles away from where your married or school life was, you don't know anyone or you struggle to make friends. It can be done and I'm more than happy to help you find out how.

What did I do? Ok, well I first moved here, and it was just me and my then to be husband, travelling around, and he had to work here and there, so I met a lot of his workmates. Ok, they were not my tribe to be, however, it was a start. We also met a few people on our travels and remain in touch with a few of them.

When it came to settling and I was able to seek work, which by the way was no laughing matter, it was one of the most stressful, soul-destroying experiences of my life. I mean I had heaps of experience working in offices, coordinating, managing, fixing and teaching with more responsibility on my shoulders than you could imagine working in the health and social sector, however, moving to another country meant that all the qualities and qualifications I had developed in this field didn't really account to much. I found this really hard to get my head around, however, I needed to work, because at this stage I still wasn't accustomed to the Australian chilled-out lifestyle.

I managed to secure a job working in disability support. So again, I had more people to mix with and have a chat to. This was at the time when we decided it was safe to lay some roots, we were going to get our own place, how exciting.

Situations, locations and improvements

As it turned out, we ended up on the coast to attend a work meeting for my husband and as soon as I arrived, I totally fell in love with the area and there and then we decided this would be our home, our settling point, so again we moved, and had to start again.

New home, new job, equals new people. So, as you see moving around can certainly have the potential for building new tribes, it doesn't have to be daunting or tragic; it can be whatever you want it to be.

I decided I wanted to be a part of a community; remember I hadn't ever really had time to create a community lifestyle for myself before, yet somehow this new life I had chosen for myself was going to be consciously different.

Making friends

I joined a neighbourhood site with an app that connected you to the local neighbourhood. I joined a coffee group and started to mingle. Unfortunately, that one didn't end well as one of the ladies in the group was quite a negative soul and created so much drama amongst the ladies that I eventually had to remove myself from her. Through the group though I have met a bunch of truly amazing women that I have in my life today and I love them all dearly.

My new job became quite a challenge too. I went through an incident that prevented me from continuing in the role I had, and the contract prevented long term employment. It entailed lots of stress and lots of therapy, and led me to push myself to start working for myself, which brought me to where I am in my business today. Plus, I've met some amazing and supportive people through that company, including my new best friend.

See how life has its ways of creating new opportunities and tribes if we just try and just do what we need to do. Anything is possible.

In my new business I now meet so many fabulous and amazing women, many from just deciding to write this book and the networking opportunities that have arisen from the very basis of that.

Starting out as a massage and holistic therapist opened up a brand-new network of clients and people in my life. People who I can share my new life with, people to teach and learn from, people to grow with, people to open up many other doors to my future, people to hug and laugh with, people to allow my gratitude and self to exist with.

Don't be afraid to find what you need to find, receive what you need to receive with your people.

If you want to thrive in a particular area in your life, if you have big dreams and goals that you want to give, if you have love and are deeply connected to the people in your world, if you are going through a challenging time in your life, such as a divorce, separation or traumatic change, the more you need deep and meaningful friendships around you to support you through the process. We have relied on other humans since the start of existence. If you manage in an independent way on a daily basis, you'll realise something is missing, you need to share and check in with your friends about your life, you need this to thrive if not to survive.

So, how do you find this new tribe, this important if not vital link to your entire existence? Well, let's start with the wonderful world of social media.

In my opinion, Facebook is one of the best and worst as far as being social, however, if used correctly you can soon find exactly what you need in your world. Facebook offers opportunities to meet up and lots of other community groups - large or small, local or distant - it doesn't matter. Communication is the key to existence. You just need to find the best suitable form of communication that sits well with your personality.

If you're in the corporate world and need connections, LinkedIn can introduce you to so many other people; and who knows, your new best friend could be hidden away just waiting to be found.

In my opinion, Twitter is less personal. I find this my great portal to the world of news and celebrities and can be very entertaining at times.

Go to a library, museum, coffee shop, shopping centre, or hobby store. Everyone needs to go to shops after all, and these are all ways of seeing people and saying hi or receiving a much-needed smile to make your day brighter.

What to do now

Offer yourself as a volunteer; there are hundreds of organisations desperately in need of other people's free time and assistance to support a cause. I did this myself - I worked for a while helping to support "the breakfast club" which was a local organisation run to help support the homeless. Giving yourself and your time is much more than meeting people; it's a way to get to know your community, the real-life effects of the community you live in, other people just like yourselves, and it is so rewarding when you're giving.

Get yourself involved. I have had clients ask me how I manage to make new friends and one particular lady asked why do we actually need them. For starters, having friends is important for brain and mental health, they help to reduce stress and keep us uplifted and strong. Having friends actually helps us heal quicker! Some ladies I've worked with have worked deeply on confidence and self-esteem, building strategies to get them feeling better about themselves before they are able to take the leap and find at least one friend.

I had to laugh when one of my clients claimed to be "weird and boring," so why would anyone want to become friends with her. She claimed she wasn't like everyone else or does what everyone else does because she's so different! Now this is my kinda gal! I so loved the fact that she recognised her own uniqueness, and as I explained to her, she was not alone, millions or at least a few other women would be waiting to befriend someone just as wonderful and weird as her. You see, her perception of who she was needed updating; she was far from boring, let me tell you.

I'm leaving this chapter with a few suggestions; firstly, go and join as many groups either online or locally as you can.

BounceBackAbility

- ❖ Make at least one new friend then journal how it felt and what type of friend you think you have created in her.

- ❖ Think about how you are going to increase or create your tribe.

- ❖ Go and have fun.

Sharing is Caring

Having a child is one of the most precious and cherished moments of your life.

All of those loving and spectacular emotions that arise from deep within you, from simply looking at your own magical creation.

From a woman's perspective

I can only give you my version of how becoming a mum or parent can feel and all those wonderful reasons I find so much passion from deep within as to why I feel us mums have a special bond with our babies.

We ladies definitely have separate and quite different attachments to our babies, and that is no criticism, just a fact of life. Even scientists have proven that our roles are intended for different purposes. Most of us wear our babies inside our own bodies like some foreign body or alien species, allowing it to grow and move around, causing many changes to our physical, psychological, mental and spiritual beings. Never mind all the vomiting, nausea, aches and pains. We need to adjust our appearance and styles to suit our ever-expanding and changing vessels. Our lifestyle changes completely – instantly - and it has to, because we need to protect the life that we need to be entirely responsible for. With that comes this massive urgency and suddenly we turn into this protective warrior that would kill anyone who threatens to cause any harm at this stage.

Baby #1 Lucy Hannah

You're feeling this again right now, aren't you? I know this because that first time will never leave your brain - ever! For me, this first pregnancy was horrible. The doctor even refused to admit I was pregnant and tried to prescribe me medication to stop my morning sickness (6.00am on the dot daily for around six months). That didn't go down well! After seeing a gynaecologist and having a scan, I was informed I was 21.5 weeks pregnant and it looked like I was carrying a healthy baby - phew! So, on May 3rd 1989, and nine days early, I gave birth to my beautiful baby girl 'Lucy Hannah,' weighing in at 6 lb 5 oz.

Baby #2 Thomas Allan

My second pregnancy was much different. I had gone to have my contraceptive coil changed after two years (as recommended), and as the doctor was placing the new one in, I passed out on the table. As it turns out, my body was rejecting it because I was already pregnant. Then came the blood tests; the count levels were not at the desired rate, so I had to go through a procedure known as an Amniocentesis, which involves using a big-ass needle and taking fluid out of your baby's sac and then testing it for down syndrome and/or any other defects, then waiting for a few weeks for the results. You're unable to lift any weight or raise your arms as this may cause harm. You need to wait again to find out if your baby is healthy or not. During this time, you need to prepare yourself for the what-ifs, if you discover anything out of the ordinary. I can assure you this is not a pleasant experience to go through. As it happened, we never made any decision and thankfully, we never had to.

The only conclusion we had on the count being abnormal is he was born huge! So, I got really large during this pregnancy and suffered with carpal tunnel syndrome and severe lower back and groin pains. My waters broke in the car on the way in, so two hours later, my nine days late, 'Thomas Allan' was born on 31st January 1992 weighing 9 lb 10 oz, full of bruises and blisters, face presentation too, which I may add was unusual at the time and I had to have a textbook delivery with around 17 students and doctors around just in case, so you can just imagine the trauma that put on me. I actually went into shock afterwards and I felt it took me longer to bond with him as I rejected him for a while at first, until I felt guilty and soon fell in love with my boy.

Baby #3 Bobby Alexander

Pregnancy and baby number three was another surprise for me. A few weeks earlier I had to take the morning after pill, because of a slip-up, however, I was having the most severe abdominal pains imaginable, so the doctor sent me to the hospital to get checked out, thinking I was having an ectopic pregnancy. After some tests it was revealed that I was normally pregnant at 5.5 weeks. You're kidding me - how is this possible? Plus, I've just had a baby six months ago. No real issues with this pregnancy, luckily, as I felt I didn't have time as I was already busy with two toddlers as it was. On time - 10th May 1993 - I gave birth to a healthy boy, 'Bobby Alexander'. He was meant to be. Going through that, all too soon I knew I had enough babies for me, so I stayed in until I had myself sterilised.

In my opinion, pregnancy/birthing and nursing on top of the whole body and lifestyle changes give you the God-given right to own that mother child bond like no other!

Being Mum

In a typical, balanced marriage a Mum is required to make certain decisions and we go through more sleepless nights than any man because we're programmed differently, we think deeper and harder about needs, we nurse and comfort a crying baby longer, we take them for their jabs or surgeries, and we choose their clothing, food, décor. The father's role is equally as important and necessary; generally they work to make sure there is enough money to pay the bills and keep you all safe and with a roof over your heads. They are to support you and balance you and make some of the other decisions that maybe us mums are too emotionally tired to make. They make girls their princesses and protect them, the boys should learn how to become a man from them, plus heaps of other stuff.

I'm simply showing you that both parents are attached and responsible for the living, human creation that both of them created and we all know that as much as that sounds like the perfect parenting guide and an ideal balance, reality is often so very far away from that very balance, which brings me to the part when you get divorced and you suddenly have to share your children!

Divorced Mum

No woman wants to lose her babies or even part with them for a minute, especially when whatever the reason they have divorced is raw and we don't trust their arses! Over our dead body are they stealing our babies. Oh yes, I admit I had all those thoughts, plus many more.

Sharing is Caring

I know what goes through the mind of most of us mums; we also really want a great moral parenting solution, and for many of us the ex doesn't always care what we want and will go out of their way to rebel or piss us right off, just to make a point (whatever that may be in their often idiotic and tiny minds)! Not only does a great one sided parenting confuse the heck out of us, the children haven't got a clue who to believe or trust, or who indeed they're supposed to learn from or look up to. This often brings massive risks of developmental issues too.

Communication has to be the key and working together whether we like each other anymore or not. How we feel for each other is irrelevant. Remember those wonderful feelings we had when we conceived? Yeah, well that shouldn't change just because two adults don't work out anymore, the baby is still here and still requires all the love from both sides. Communication and acceptance; you need to find a way, whatever way works for you both, fighting aside and for fuck's sake don't be using these poor babies as pawns or as point scorers - seriously grow the fuck up! Accept you're adults and the child matters. Yes, that is right, the child matters!

You can do all your screaming and performing, crying to the point of meltdowns, tantrums and breakdowns all you like, just do it out of sight of these babies; they don't need to see that shit. I'm all about honesty and openness with our babies, but you've gotta draw the line somewhere haven't you? This doesn't exactly instil the makings of moral and legal rights of both parents.

Think about setting down some rules. Maybe learn a few boundaries and stick to them. Have your own rules at each other's homes and don't interfere with each other's; for one it's none of your business what they do at Dads unless of course it is a case of neglect or fear, then yes step the fuck right in. Be prepared for the hard part as none of this is going to be easy. Be ready mentally as it's going to test you as a human on all levels as it is, never mind as a mum.

Child's play

When I say prepare yourself for the difficult parts, I mean the games, and the play offs, and that's just the children! It doesn't take long for them to know how to play and which buttons to press, all for a little extra attention, because they need to be involved and they still believe both parents need to be together somehow so causing shit creates a meeting, which puts them together!

Even for a few minutes, your emotions and patience will be tested to the max. Don't fall for it; just keep your eyes and ears open and be a step ahead. Us women are pretty clever at this, so it shouldn't be tasking, unless, of course your usually sensible child decides to be devious and play the game too. So, get some boundaries ready and wait for the tests; they will come!

Another tip; if you are at a sharing stage, please don't fall into the trap of needing to impress them on your shift. Kids need to feel as normal as possible and not be bought or overfed, and that's not just food! Kids need some downtime too, time to chill out with each parent, it's exhausting for them to try and make it fit wherever they are. Think about it, split homes, broken routines and trying to please both sets of parents, not to mention any add-ons to the families.

Moral ground

A big no-no is to bag or name-call the ex in front of or to your children. Seriously, what picture of yourself do you want to paint to your own flesh and blood? They will always follow your direction, so if you want your babies to have great moral standards as they grow into adulthood then you have to show them how that's done. Show them you care and be understanding. How would you feel hearing someone say bad things about you or your own parent? Think about that for a moment too.

Sharing is Caring

As babies grow, they soon learn for themselves and develop their own opinions or judgements. Give them the opportunity to learn that part for themselves. Please do not use your babies as a ditching station for your emotional release. I'm not saying hide all your feelings from them, however, they are not professionals nor your best friends, so they don't need the burden or pressure any more than they have already.

Try and plan regular talks or family meetings. I can tell you, older kids hate these, but I found them really useful, as it brings everything to the table and no one can play each parent off as much, because you're all there together and you've gotta face each other. It's especially helpful and healthier if you have extended families and you're all present. It may sound too good to be true, or even a nightmare but trust me it's so much nicer when you're all on the same page. In my day there were no apps for communicating and arranging co-parenting, so we had to work it out as we went along.

Sharing

If you do manage to share and the co-parenting gets on its way, you're offering your babies stability, and both parents having a role to play in their life gives you some relief of pressure. Having children is challenging at the best of times, so doing it all on your own is no ball game. Trust me, I had my feel of that for quite some time too; it's not pleasant, it's highly stressful and you get no medals or thanks for the extra slog you put in. What's worse is, when you're struggling to hold the family together with a roof over your head and the ex is playing great Dad with his new partner's children, and you see the pain in their eyes.

There is a plus with sharing though; as you get used to it and the babies grow up and accept this is the norm, you get free time to do something for yourself for once, like have adult fun, even if fun to you means laying at home in control of the remote and going to sleep earlier without laying there worrying what time the kids roll in way after the deadline.

If you don't work it out, then you're responsible for the adults you create. Ok, not entirely all of the adult they become, but you will contribute to a confused one who can end up with abandonment and development issues, as I said earlier, left craving for attention or affection, and hold a whole lot of resentment and blame for one or both you parents. Are you really prepared for that?

My way

I don't believe for one minute that I did it the right way all the way through my parenting years, but it wasn't for the will of trying. I know how difficult it is when you're being manipulated and even threatened if you should, God forbid, want to receive your fair share of child maintenance to stay at home and raise the children because he wants to work 24/7 for the future that never materialises.

I also know what it's like not being allowed to keep your family in the comfort of their own home, as I had to leave with all three children and to rent a scabby house miles away. Unable to drive, we had to travel over an hour morning and evening every day because I wanted to keep some stability in their lives by keeping them in their schools. It was a massive struggle to make it work and once things settled and I met husband number two we moved away from the area.

Regardless of the upheaval and challenges moving away and starting new schools in a new area, we managed to make the transition and blend both the families quite smoothly. We tried a few different sharing options and came to a mutual option that would work for us all, so every other weekend we had them and vice versa. This way I got the luxury of being a mum and doing family stuff, then a weekend to do fun adult stuff, and so did their dad.

Holidays and school events were also taken into account and for many years this was still jointly attended to. We got to a place where both families blended and communicated so well.

When changes occur

I recall many coffee dates at each other's houses and I even looked after my ex-husband's new partner's children. It was really pleasant and healthy for everyone, which was why it was a shame that their relationship should end, as the next partner he chose was nothing like this. In fact, it created an entire separation as he was no longer allowed to be friends with me, and the children didn't feel happy there anymore; they felt left out all the time. She had her own children and a very tight family so my babies became my babies and not so much ours anymore. I still believe this changed the entire relationship and attitude of my then ever-growing babies; along came behaviour issues that often got so out of control I had no idea how to cope. And as much as their father was a control freak on a power mission most of the time, his way of dealing with them clearly didn't work either. Losing that trust and friendship changed the dynamics of our previously well-working co-parenting.

The ugly

Later when another marriage failed due to constant cheating, we had to move again; this time closer to my friends as I needed that support, and the old school and their father, to hopefully build up a closer working relationship again. For a few years it was ok and both dad and stepdad, along with their families, remained active in their lives and for a while it seemed great, apart from the fact that actually all this moving around from one family home to another on each visit was taking its toll. The children became resentful for being away from their friends and started to rebel. I knew it was all a huge part in growing up and building resilience, I should know all about that, however, these were my babies and I wanted them to have a stable, loving life.

So, my next relationship started out as a bit of fun, and I made it quite clear I didn't need another daddy replacement for my babies; this was supposed to be for me. This is where I say be very careful what you wish for, because the universe listens, and that is exactly what I got; eight years of me and my babies versus me and my fella. Sounds fab in a way doesn't it? Well it's far from fab in reality, because he officially moved in to my home after three years, and that was a strain because he would only move in on the condition that he went on the mortgage that I had secured for myself and my babies, but I agreed and, in many ways, I regret making that move, because eventually I had to sell it and we gained nothing, except I got the freedom from the release.

Anyway, these years together in the same house with then teenagers was a freaking nightmare at times. I had to work full-time in a heavily responsible and stressful office, keep the kids busy, clothed and fed, obviously as well as keep the peace at home. There were never any joint trips out or sit down family dinners; the tension in the house could be cut with a knife. It was a constant battle for me to keep this as balanced as I could for them.

Living with a Jekyll and Hyde doesn't help matters when he had control of the TV and sofa. The children weren't even allowed to be in there if he was, otherwise he would complain about noise or anything they did. Out socialising he was the funniest guy you'd meet and that's what kept us together that long. I know it sounds selfish, but I was still searching for a perfect family life. And you get to the point of believing this is as good as it gets; I made my bed so I must lie in it. I'm sure you've heard so many variations of this.

Being the child of divorce and abuse

Maybe I got that attitude or mind frame because I had been at the other end of the scale; as a child of divorce myself I saw some nasty stuff as a kid living in the constant dramas of my own parent's shit that made me crave and protect, or at least try, so much.

I know when I went through it how I felt; never knowing if or when I'd see a Mum or Dad. I clung on to my baby brother and sister when we were together. I remember being around eight years old and no parents to be found; the neighbours were the only ones around.

I recall an occasion when one neighbour came and fed us the fat out of the chip pan! On another occasion we were sat in her room and she fed us baked beans while they sat with a cooked dinner. We watched a carnival on TV that I had been promised to attend by my dad, and I was so sad.

I used to have the strangest of dreams. One recurring dream was about nuns who took my mother and brought her back many years later. I had that dream into adulthood and feared nuns until recently.

There would be teenage boys caring (if you want to call it that) for us. I won't go into details, but things happened that shouldn't happen to any child. But I was rather it be me than my siblings. The abuse became normal for me, however, no one was going to get to my babies – ever!

I remember going to school and being given breakfast by the headmistress in her office and getting a round of applause when I returned to a school after being in a battered wives home with my mum for a period of time.

I remember the other kids at school talking about me and picking on me because I smelt or had dirty knickers on, moving school and home after home, never getting time to make any friends. I know many of you will sit and think, well back in the day things were tough and that's the way it was, and maybe you're thinking SO WHAT? And you're absolutely right, so what indeed, life is life and shit happens. But this crap of a childhood actually built me to be the strong woman I am today and I have to say I'd like my own children to realise why I was, and still am, the Mum I am today.

What to do

So, you see there is a right and a wrong way of how to share your babies. Each of us have our own issues and situations. I'm not here to judge; how could I? We do a good enough job of that on ourselves, don't we? However, please always remember that baby you both created still counts.

Questions I'm faced with by many divorced women are, "I carried this baby so my bond is greater than his and more important," "the dad doesn't know the kids like I do," they're at work all day so it makes sense for me to have them full-time," "the kids don't like going to their house," and as you may have worked out I have answered all of those within this chapter.

At the end of the day, as long as you do your best, what more can you do? Children will still grow up and be resentful about something you did or didn't do as a parent- right or wrong - regardless, and they will often aim to do parenting totally different to you! Take on board and find a way that's right for you and your babies, and don't judge what's already been and gone; you did the best you could with the knowledge you had at the time.

Sharing is Caring

- ❖ Co-parenting/joint custody apps are available - I'd recommend for an easier and sharing wisely way to get through this is to use them.

- ❖ Commit to making some co-parenting rules and boundaries and please be realistic about them and both stick to them if you want what's best for you all.

- ❖ If the dad doesn't want to know or participate - screw him, you can't force him and that's ok too; all will work out fine in the end.

- ❖ Talk openly to your babies, show them you love them no matter what, show them all the love and support they need. Just keep those eyes wide open for all the guilt trips and play offs!

Honouring yourself

"Daring to set boundaries is about having the courage to love ourselves, even when we risk disappointing others".
Brene Brown

Mind your own bloody business, it's got nothing to do with you. Now that should be the attitude you have when it comes to how you view the lives of others as well as your own.

Your own shit is your only concern

Tending to your own garden and thinking about what goes on in your own life is a priority and not a selfish act. When you fill your time tending to your own stuff and not sticky-beaking your way through what others are doing with their stuff, you'll benefit in more ways than you could possibly imagine. Remember to set your own fence around yourself and concentrate on what goes in there. This is a boundary; I dare you to give it a go!

The way you act and treat yourself sends out massive, super-bright in-your-face signals to predators, and this alerts them with permission to treat you exactly the same way. Try not to send out the signs that read, "I'm a doormat," as that is an opening for others to walk all over you or dismiss you as if you're not even there, causing you to be pushed aside or pushed around without even noticing it. Then, before you know it, you're going to follow a path of destruction, as well as continuing to attract the wrong men, people and friends into your life, and it will all be your own fault. I know it sounds a bit harsh, but it's true; only you get to control how you're treated. Let's face it, it's your responsibility. So, what do you plan on doing about it? Accepting it or changing it?

Start setting healthy boundaries

Honouring yourself by setting some healthy boundaries will set out the standards you have for yourself, your ethics and your morals. This is a huge part of who you are, or at least who you want to be if you're not quite there yet because of the nasty patterns you've created in your own life, plus it's because of the learnt memories you've grown up with.

It's not entirely all your fault how you got to the stage of how you are today, or at least were before the day of recognition; we all get to that actual point of enough is enough, don't we? When my pitfall hit me, I knew I couldn't carry on anymore; I had to do something to stop allowing all the abuse and dramas to continue to eat away at my very existence. My day of recognition was on 19th December 2014 and how I got there eventually didn't even matter in the end; the important and crucial part is the how do we change it and what do we do next?

Honouring yourself

Setting your own rules, boundaries and standards are up to you. This is your job, so I'd think really carefully about the type of life you really, honestly and truly want for yourself and then start there. Go right down to the basics and write a list of all the things you like and dislike about how you feel when you're treated a certain way, or watch how others are being treated and maybe, just maybe you already recognise how you're being treated and you realise you just don't like it anymore. Wouldn't that be a great revelation? Only you know what you want for yourself, so think about what's not right for you, think about how people around you talk to you.

Don't forget to get it all journaled. Take these lists, because I'm guessing there are a whole lot of them. Ground yourself or take yourself to a quiet spot and take a long and hard look at those lists. What do you see? What are you feeling? What would you like to change?

Observations and actions

Do you have a friend or two who talks about others in a totally disrespectful manner, yet you don't feel the same? Do you just accept that? Note to yourself - whatever way these friends of yours are talking; disrespecting, gossiping or foul-mouthing others, they're doing exactly the same about you to them, so don't be disillusioned to believe you're so special or any different that they wouldn't do that to you, or believe you're worshipped and respected, yet no one else is. Wake up darlings - do you really want friends in your life with that attitude? You can start by not wanting to hear someone say bad things about someone else to you, by saying to the said friend, "hey I know you have that opinion of….(whoever that may be), but please don't tell me anymore as I don't feel the same as you on that matter," or, "I don't feel comfortable listening". You can add that as much as you value their friendship, you don't wish to be involved. Maybe you could try sitting back and not responding or giving any answer or reactions as this can be as equally powerful if you're not comfortable speaking up. At least acting this way is an amazing step in the right direction for you, as you need to start setting your own boundaries.

By adding this boundary you'll start to send out the signals that you're not accepting this kind of behaviour, and you'll see that it won't come your way as often. You can use this method in all other areas of your life too without dramas, upsets or fall outs, and you can start to eliminate all those toxic people from your life quietly.

I've got so damn good at this in my life I feel like I'm an expert in this now. If I'm not feeling comfortable or feeling a good energy from someone around me, or I don't want someone in my life anymore, they're gone. I simply remove myself and make it my choice to not involve myself in their presence anymore.

Simple, but not always easy for everyone. It's easy for me now because I've learnt to appreciate myself and my worth. I've learnt to value myself enough now to be able to choose who shares my energy fields and my precious time. I feel so fortunate to have created this place where I attract some absolutely fabulous people into my world, and you can do that too. I know many of you reading this will have an armful of excuses, but come and work with me, I can teach you the right mindset and attitude to care so damn much about yourself you'll be able to implement this into your lives too.

Yes or No?

Take back the control of your own life, stop allowing yourself to back down and accept it's ok because you don't want conflict, because it's not.

Honouring yourself

One thing you don't need to have is conflict and that's the beauty of setting boundaries, because it can be as basic or full on as you choose. Just relearn how to say yes and no, and don't just say these words because that's pretty obvious, get yourself into the habit of knowing what to say yes or no to and when to say yes and no. Try to be less of a no person if you're a yes person - just saying that sounds hypercritical, doesn't it?

So, if you always say yes because you want to be a people-pleaser or you're not doing stuff because you really want to, then start saying no more often. Eventually the habit kicks in and you'll be a professional at only saying yes to all the wonderful stuff you'll feel great about and vice versa.

For those of you who constantly say no to joining in or helping out in fear of being seen as a fun, caring or generous individual, not forgetting the fear of failing and being judged, then start by saying yes and get a life, a life that you want to really have, a life that sits well with your soul, a life you're happy and proud to live. No hiding, blocking or refusing yourself.

Mind attracts mind, like attracts like and so on. We are magnets to our surroundings by our own beliefs and actions. You should think about that, it's true, take pride in the decisions you make, the choices you make, feel that sense of empowerment knowing you've made a choice that you're totally more than ok with. Blimey, imagine feeling that sense of happiness and pride every single day of your life, just because you decided enough was enough, no more controlling outside influencers, no more manipulators, no more fear of refusing people in your life. You have the power to have this right inside yourself here and now.

Choose how you want to be

If you don't do anything about it then that's fine, you can just carry on living the life you are doing. After all, that is your choice too, and maybe you're happy plodding along this way. I'm not knocking it, or throwing judgement at you, it's your life after all, it doesn't affect mine. If you're happy to live as you are then that's wonderful too, just be sure you're not being a people-pleaser or a doormat; make sure you're happy with being co-dependant. Be prepared for later on when you're living a life with repressed emotions; just prepare yourself to continue feeling angry, shameful and bitter because that's all, and I don't want to imagine anyone of you out there having to feel that way.

I had no boundaries, nor did I ever honour myself in the past. I literally did learn the hard way, as you've probably worked out by now, growing up and being surrounded by very strong characters, plus the toxic and abusive people around me. I actually didn't know any different, so I accepted it all, took it all on. I didn't say I liked it, in fact far from it, which is what led me to be resentful, shameful, carrying hurt so much. I hid my true self, I didn't know what I liked or who I really was, I continually attracted drama and chaos, and all along I had no idea I was responsible for it, not that I had the power to change it. How ironic is that, all the answers to the whys and how's were inside me all along, I just had to take a step and listen to the inner self then read all the signs. It's not as if I hadn't been given enough hints, after all.

So, as you can see, setting my own boundaries didn't happen at the start of my journey to live a healthier life, I had to do plenty of soul searching and work with other coaches and mentors to show me how to unveil why I was attracting all this. I tell you something, once I got that kick up the butt, and that reality check, the ending is amazing. I actually do know what I want and who I want in my life, so now I'm still able to remove toxic people from my life, just now I'm able to manifest much healthier relationships and allow only what fits into my moral and self-loving, non-toxic, non-chaotic, awesome life.

A little tip - visualise yourself living a protected, loving life without any dramas or concerns for what anyone else is doing with their lives. Imagine the inner peace right now. Sing out beautiful and meaningful affirmations such as, "with love you can keep your emotions and I shall keep only mine". Go on, try it.

So, start to be honest with yourself and open up about what you really feel. It doesn't haven't be done with contempt; you can easily express your wishes for a healthier relationship by using lines like, "I'm not comfortable with that", "it doesn't feel good to….","I'm not okay with …", "I appreciate if you wouldn't…", "please don't…", or, like I said earlier, just take a step back and don't respond at all. Or instead of words, body language works; just nod or shake your head, or better still, use your hands to gesture. There are so many non-confrontational ways to start.

You've heard the Roy Orbison song, "Silence is Golden"? Well, in this case it can be.

It all takes time, patience and practice, just keep in mind that this is your life and you're entitled to live it your own way with your own standards and boundaries. Once you learn to love and respect yourself enough, you'll gain more confidence to set them and protect yourself.

Know your boundaries

The boundaries I set myself include the physical, which is my personal space. I love hugs and I'm very touchy-feely, but that's me and it's not for everyone. So, for you I'd say think about how you want your own physical boundaries met. I have a friend who cringes if you go to hug and kiss her, so I respect her boundaries and give her a pat! No, not like a dog, before you think that's acceptable, even though I sneakily get the rare short hugs when she's up for it.

My emotional boundaries still get tested on a regular basis, and I'm ok with that too. As the vocal, opinionated being that I am, I've learnt to accept others being just like me, so I'm ok with listening to what others have to say. The difference with me is I would never say anything to deliberately hurt or offend other people's feelings; partly because I'm respectful of others and partly because I know how much it hurts me, so why would I want to hurt anyone else? I believe we treat others in a way we would want to be treated ourselves, and I love to be loved. The fact that I have always accepted others for who they are made me an easy target for abusers, and that's ok, I'm not changing who I am, I'm just changing the fact that I am choosier as to who I accept in my world.

I know anger is a tough one to hold back on; often we lash out or shout as we need to release these emotions. So, my advice here is to get that anger and go and scream in a pillow, or scream out a song as loud as you can. This releases the same emotions, just on a healthier level.

Other boundaries that are to be looked at and worked on are our intellectual boundaries. You'll be amazed how many partners, friends, acquaintances and work colleagues forget that this is a need to be met and not presume it's ok to intimidate or be intimidated, or even holding back advice knowledge or information.

Sexual boundaries. Again, know what you're comfortable with. It is not acceptable to just take innuendo or propositions. I spent my life living with this one, with no boundaries whatsoever, and as much as I am highly sexual and very open and experimental about this, I have learnt what's right and wrong and what I am willing to accept, and I'm not afraid to say no.

Honouring yourself

Material boundaries. This is similar to financial boundaries. I always had an uncomfortable relationship with money and didn't ever like to talk about money. I was afraid of it, even ashamed to mention it. How mad does that sound now? In fact, I only recently learnt to love money and not to be afraid to want it or use it or accept it into my life openly. And hey, after working with a spiritual prosperity teacher, I'm embracing the pennies and spending them equally and lovingly without having the mindset of having to work my knuckles to the bone and depriving myself of any luxuries. I'm also easily giving; my money mindset is the universe will see you give, so will give you back in abundance, and so she does.

Time boundaries. This is where you value your own time and set a high price on how you spend or how you give it. I was always proud of being a giver and my time I felt was free and easy, so I actually got to a point of being worn out. Now I make myself unavailable so I can manage my time to suit my needs. Yes, I sometimes say no to social gatherings, but I catch up later and I get quality time in return. I don't give my time away for nothing anymore; I give my time with value. I am precious about using my time wisely and if I feel I need more me time, then that's exactly what I give myself, and guess what, I definitely do not allow myself to feel guilty about it.

Human rights

If you haven't heard of the Human Rights Act, I strongly urge you to look it up and see how you should and shouldn't allow yourself to be treated, or treat others. So, for now I'll give you some of the basic human rights that are internationally recognised and legally bound.

Rights to equality

Freedom from discrimination

Right to life, liberty and personal security

Freedom from torture and degrading treatment

Right to recognition as a person before the law

Right to equality before the law

Right to a public hearing

Right to rest and leisure

Freedom of opinion and information

Right to marriage and family

Right to adequate living standard

Freedom of belief and religion

Plus, many more. So, as you can see, it is not only for your own state of mind and lifestyle, it is the law to be treated with respect, dignity and fairness. No-one has the right to take your choices away from you, nor judge you and your beliefs.

What to do now

"What is setting boundaries?" As I've stated earlier, setting boundaries is creating a list of the standards in which you choose to live by.

"How do I start setting them?" Firstly, you have to start with the basics of discovering what you like and dislike in all areas of your life; mentally physically and emotionally. And this is a big task to set about, but essential in setting boundaries and moving forward in your life.

Honouring yourself

"You say I need to learn to say no. I find this so hard to do as I'm afraid I will upset someone else's feelings or they might get angry with me." My whole point to here, saying no may seem as a negative and an often confrontational response, however, think about this - surely if you're not really wanting to do something, and you're happy to say yes only to please someone else, how does this look to you when you're so easily saying no to yourself? To me this is not an act of kindness, this is not showing yourself the respect and love you deserve, so there are some steps to saying no you can take that will make saying no easier in time. This is you shoving yourself down the pecking order, and if you're going to do this to yourself, then you have to expect others to do this to you too!

"How do I know if my boundaries have been crossed?" Get to know whether you're comfortable or not and someone has crossed your boundaries by listening to your body. By this I mean if someone acts or says something to you, how are you feeling? Tired, upset, knots in stomach? Your heart misses a beat, or you feel tight or anxious? Butterflies in your stomach? These are the signs your body is giving you as a way of telling you something, what you have to do is work out what that is. Then go from there.

- ❖ Write yourself a list of likes and dislikes and think about how it's looking for you.

- ❖ Journal down all of your yes's for a week, take a look at them and think about what you wanted to say no to. Maybe flip it over and try it with no's. On reflection, how does that feel?

- ❖ Do you love yourself enough to start a boundaries list?

- ❖ Some additional support or learnings for you would be to watch Brene Brown, The Call to Courage, read an awesome book named Boundaries by Dr Henry Cloud and Dr John Townsend, and Co-dependant by Melody Beattie.

In the Words of my Little Sis

"The Greatest gifts our parents ever gave us was each other."

Unknown

Having a sister and brother to care for when you're still young yourself places huge responsibilities on your shoulders. It totally defines you and changes a pattern that determines how you live your entire life.

Which is what I was later to discover. However, life was difficult for us and we were separated so many times in our lives; we have still a connection that will never be broken. On reflection, I wouldn't change anything because this is why we are who we are, and although we lost our brother to drugs in 2010, my sister and I still remain. Our early years obviously were mapped out on similar paths, regardless of how very different we perceive life. Now as adults and observing how the first 50 years of our lives has moulded us, I discovered in our own ways we both lived in the footsteps of our own parent's chaotic and unstable life that led to divorce. So, I thought it would be a wonderful idea to ask my little sister how she saw how her life took her, in regards to bouncing back and getting through life and the divorces she has experienced herself. Typing her words cut deep into my heart.

Her story

Hello, my name is Zena. My life has had many standstills. I don't know really where to start, so let's go back to the beginning. I was born on 9th August 1970 and have an elder sister and a younger brother.

Life in the 70's and 80's was very hard for us, especially looking back on everything that was going on around us and to us, so I managed to block a lot of my younger life out. It was in my youth that I realised I wasn't being the confident girl I dreamt I would be as life was really hard with a very strict upbringing.

Moving from one parent to another then back again too had its tolls, and to top it off I had a speech impediment, so communication was really difficult for me. Like life itself wasn't bad enough, I felt like I was living in this difficult world on my own.

By the time I was 15 years old and I hated it all including myself, the only person I ever remember as a mother figure was my big sister to me and my then little brother. Even she was taken away from me. We were a dysfunctional family with tight boundaries and hardened rules; not what I had hoped my life would have been.

Doing as I was told

When I was 18 years old my mum arranged and made me go on a date I didn't want to go on. I just wanted to stay at home and do my usuals; study my college work, eat, do the household chores and sleep, because that's what we were told to do. We did exactly as we were told in those days too, so there was no room for play or social activities. I did as I was told and dated this man who was six years older than me. He ended up becoming my boyfriend after a couple of approved dates from my mum.

The bonus was, he said my short tongue suited me and he liked it, so I started to feel good about myself with him. It wasn't long before I found myself pregnant with our first child. He said we would get married, so in just six weeks that's what we did. I didn't know any different, so I did as I was told. So being Mrs Ganson made life a bit better for me at first, until he became controlling. I soon became emotionally and mentally drained. I planned my second pregnancy because he didn't want any more children but I did. I needed to have babies, but he wanted me to terminate it. I couldn't and didn't. Life was doable but it took 11 years before it ended in divorce - and it was a nasty one too - but I knew I needed out and to be free. I needed to find a piece of myself.

Number two

After taking a job as a cleaner at a power station a year later, I tried to fix my friend up with someone there. She let me down and didn't turn up, and as I didn't want to stay at home alone, bored again, and be just a depressed stay at home mum of two, I decided to go instead.

To my surprise, he turned out to be my next new man and I soon fell pregnant. Along came a baby girl; she was our world, we were so happy. I had it all; a new man, a new home and a new baby. All was fantastic and looking bright. We weren't living together but life was pretty perfect. We got engaged and planned our wedding. He stood up and accepted my first two children, then when my third baby girl was just six weeks old, I fell pregnant again. So then came baby number four. Our world was starting to feel complete now and life was starting to feel amazing. We had a huge church wedding, then only five days after our wedding, my new husband Garry had to return to Ireland to work.

I later received an email saying that he couldn't offer me anything - that was it, done, over five days, so one year later the divorce came through. There were no problems, the divorce sailed by and there I was left alone again and this time with four children. He continued to see his children a few times a year at first, then that slowly stopped, so I had a few years on my own, and I was happy. I had my babies and one of them I had discovered had special needs.

I took solace in decorating my home.

Number three

I spoilt my children, but they were good kids and tried their best. Every other weekend my eldest two would go to their nana and grandad's house to stay. They played an active and important part in their lives and have helped me so many times with them. They kind of took over the role that their own father should have, yet he was not around, so yes it was hard, but we got through it.

One day I was brushing my hair when a man looked through my front window. He was walking around the grass verge for hours. I thought this was funny to watch, and after some time, I realised I knew who his family was, and I invited him in for a cup of tea. We got talking and that continued for months and we were getting closer and closer, yet he was nine years younger than me. I don't know what I was thinking but things with him were different.

We got married, actually twice, but that's another story. I had paid for the wedding and the honeymoon. We went overseas and took the children with us. It was ok but not brilliant. I made the most of it, sitting by the pool, dancing, sunbathing and doing the normal family things that you do on a holiday.

It wasn't long before he became different; moody, irritable, controlling, violent. He was drinking heavily and doing drugs. Not the kind of life I had nor wanted for myself or my children. I don't ask anyone for help, especially my family, yet I've had help from my half-sister, and my big sister had always had my back. They have always helped me with my kids when I've needed them to. Some days he was good and others I'd end up calling the police up to three times a night.

His behaviour wasn't fair on me, my kids, or my work. He would mess the house up, smoke drugs and just do what he wanted to do and not be involved as my husband and a family man. He wasn't acting like a stepdad nor a husband, so things went from bad to worse. We broke up and I filed for divorce. He would constantly walk past my house shouting, "I love you long time". It was so embarrassing and humiliating for me; it got so bad that the police used to pick him up and just let him out of the van around the corner.

So, enough was enough. I put an end to it all. He wouldn't move out, so I moved in with the girls in their bedroom. He would bring people in the house, running up and down the stairs and in and out the bedrooms. I didn't like it; my life was spiralling out of control. One day I just paid for a taxi to take him away and that was the end of that.

Number four

My children started to attend a group that was suitable for special needs and chill out with other siblings. The children really enjoyed it there, especially my son with special needs, so I started to volunteer there and help with the crafts.

I got on really well with my boss, yet after a year he left the centre. We arranged to meet for a farewell drink and from there we started a secret relationship. I felt great because finally I was treated like a princess, and he already had developed a wonderful relationship with my children So, within a year we got engaged and started to arrange our wedding. It started to become difficult because he began having health issues, and then blood clots; that's why we married earlier. Then two weeks after our wedding we moved into my sister's house and started a real family life and the kids were settled now and we all seemed happy for once.

A few months later the illness worsened, and he started to get really poorly. We eventually discovered that he had cancer and then came the controlling behaviour at times (I seem to attract this don't I?). Life got frustrating and wasn't so good, but I knew I had to stand by him; he was starting to deteriorate and was dying in front of my eyes at home, so all his family and us were together. While this was going on my daughter had a baby. She was too young and not managing well, so I looked after him too. The relationship bonded between my sick husband and our grandson and they became close. This seemed to remove some of the stress created from going through to get a court order to care for him permanently, however, it still took its toll.

We finally said goodbye and he went to rest in peace in March 2017. I found this very hard and struggled to deal with it at first as I didn't know what to do or what to say, and for the last few months of his life my cousin was at my side and managed to keep me going throughout this awful ordeal. His family were also constantly around and I felt really close to them for about a year, but then I was dropped and soon deleted by them completely. I had my grandson to care for, but still I became lonely again.

My youngest daughter used to go clubbing and through this, someone from one of the clubs text me. I didn't want to talk to anyone at the time never mind a man, but that's when we started talking.

Number five

In January 2018 I went to Ireland with my son to his dad's house, to meet his new wife and introduce him to his grandson. Ireland was cold and wet, yet it was a holiday for my son and grandson, plus me, as it happens, as we had a whale of a time. While I was there, the man I mentioned from the club was contacting me three times a day. I had tried to block him and not get feelings because as a bouncer or doorman at bars and clubs for around 25 years, I felt he would have a reputation that I certainly wouldn't want to be part of.

Having said that, he seemed really nice, so I invited him for a cup of tea. I soon started to grow real feelings and as we got closer, I just knew that this was the first time I had real feelings for someone, just for me. I knew my life was now full of love, light and joy and I feel this will remain the same for the rest of my life.

Two years on and we are so in love with each other; there is no violence, he accepts me and loves me for just being me and doesn't want anything more than that from me. There is no controlling and although we live in separate houses at the moment, we stay at each other's all the time. We are engaged, and one day in a couple of years, we shall get married. I am just so happy that I let him into my life and not let my life slip away. My dreams, my hopes of true love and complete happiness have finally come true. I love that I chose to never give up on myself completely. We now have our children and grandchildren on both sides, and we love them all as much as we love each other.

Big Sis talking

I am so proud of my little sister for sharing her story. She mentioned she had a speech impediment, which we used to pick on her for as we were growing up as we thought it was funny. She is also dyslexic and has struggled in the education sector. She has spent life trying to please everyone else at her own expense, just like me, looking for love and doing as she "was told". I can vouch for how much of a terrible sacrifice to ourselves that has been.

You see how the same life pattern had formed for us both; having been born to the same parents with the same background and the same experiences yet living and growing up separately. There is no escaping that this is living proof of the effect divorce and abuse has on children.

I'm grateful she too has finally found a way to love herself and find her true happy place.

Freedom to Believe

"To have confidence in the truth, the existence or the reliability of something without absolute proof it's right."

Definition of Belief, Dictionary

"If you don't trust yourself then who will you trust?"

"The more you trust, the more you love, and the less you'll need to compare."

"To believe is to have something worth living for. Once the belief has gone, you are no more."

Zelda Marsh

To think is to believe.

Trust has to be one of the most powerful forms of feelings that open you up to a world of emotions, and some of the harshest you'll ever want to experience.

Trust

Trust is an emotion and a logical act where you expose your vulnerabilities to people, believing that they won't take advantage of your openness. That's huge - that's total commitment to ourselves - that's ownership to ourselves, our hearts and minds.

Without trust there is no point; there's nothing else left is there? I strongly believe that you need to start by completely allowing yourself to trust in yourself first, only then shall you be able to create a real honest belief. It is so difficult to own and earn, however it's the easiest thing to lose, and once it's gone, it can be gone forever unless you change the way you think.

Trust and the emotions associated with trust include companionships, friendships, love agreement, comfort and relaxation. You allow yourself all this with trust; how freeing does that sound? You can't build relationships without trust. If you don't trust, you're keeping yourself unavailable to others, in fact you're neglecting others' rights to you as much as your own rights to others. Trust brings loyalty. In fact, trust is loyalty. Why deprive yourself of loyalty, freedom and love?

Belief is another powerful tool that you need to utilise effectively and carefully. This can quite easily be taken over by co-dependency, which is when your own thoughts or beliefs are made by someone else, and that you've been programmed to believe instead of self-learnt. And it's not even your own fault, you can't just not know what you've already been taught, but what you can do, with lots of patience and trust, is unlearn these beliefs and thoughts, along with upskilling your knowledge and opening your heart and mind.

Imagine yourself actually living with the freedom to trust and believe in what you want to, instead of being brainwashed or co-dependant on others' memories and lessons. It will open up amazing new opportunities for you, and all of those shiny new doors will suddenly be opening and closing. This time you'll choose the right ones for you.

You gotta have faith

Do you follow a faith or religion? If you do, that's amazing, as everyone needs some support system and somewhere they can turn to or rely on. A bit like having your tribe, right? Having a faith can help you to regain trust and belief again, especially when you have lost faith and you're still pointing the finger of blame for why your marriage or relationship didn't work out how you planned, or one of you didn't follow all the wedding vows so now you're riddled with guilt and shame and find it hard to face and trust in them again.

Putting some trust in your own God or spiritual leader, for me the divine/universe who has always had my back and knows what is best for me. Your own faith/God knows how your journey is supposed to be mapped out, then the bitterness will ease and the faith and trust will begin to grow again. We all need something or someone. And you know, once you do start to gain trust in yourself you watch how everything else grows in other areas of your life too, in fact you'll become more intuitive, even your instincts will sharpen. I know this may seem a bit far-fetched to some of you, but honestly all this is real, it all comes.

I know this, not only through my own experiences, but through the observations I've made of many others who have finally trusted in themselves. I've witnessed the change in charisma and confidence in so many and I'll tell you right now, that is priceless. Intuition is so underrated; you know it's an actual proven power that us women often take for granted and many more of us even ignore – either consciously or subconsciously. Please understand that you were given this amazing gift for a reason. Don't waste it - use it to create a much happier version of yourself, as well as improve how you view your surroundings and the world with all it holds. It brings us much gratitude and positivity.

Ignoring your faith and choosing to take on others' opinions and beliefs instead of your own can and will eventually cause you to lose any shred of hope you may have for your own future, let alone anyone else's you care about. I don't know about you, but I don't really feel comfortable with allowing other people's opinions control my mind or any of the decisions I have for my own life anymore. Your functionality will weaken and for any of you who have already experienced this, you'll understand the dreary and tiresome outcomes. You'll keep holding on to negative thoughts and remain living a life of doubt and regret. This is not a happy and joyous place to be, so instead think of all the wondrous things you'll miss out on, by simply deceiving yourself and not owning your own faith and belief. You'll remain on the same pattern of thought throughout your entire existence, living a life of doubt and regret, and that doesn't look very appealing to me.

Self-talk

Did you know that you only ever believe what you tell yourself, and the more you tell it the more likely you're going to make it happen? That refers to both positive and negative thoughts and beliefs, so doesn't it make sense to tell yourself more of the good stuff – and often?

Let's face it, if someone tells you a list of 10 things they love and dislike about you - and there are nine wonderful reasons to love you and one thing they don't quite like about you, what do you think you're going to hang on to and believe the most? Yes, the one negative reason. The one tiny percentage of all the wonderful reasons will be at the bottom of what you'll allow yourself to believe. Your choice, so remember, believe what you want.

Constantly tell yourself some beautiful affirmations and make all your self-talk count.

Epiphany

Have any of you ever experienced an epiphany? If you have, I would love to hear yours. I'm about to reveal to you my latest epiphany. All year I had been experiencing some bizarre dreams and past revelations through healing sessions and meditations. A particularly weird encounter for me was during these nights I'd wake up at stupid o'clock to the noises of engines or motors and I'd be feeling like I was not really there; there being in my bed in my body, yet not being able or even wanting to move. I would have strange thoughts about the universe and aliens going on in my head, then in the morning I'd not be able to get out of bed properly as I was aching all over like I'd done a massive workout or been thrown around like a ragdoll. I was putting this down to all the emotional releases I was having or my age, and I can confirm that I was not on any medication nor touched alcohol all year, so that ruled that out.

Three days before my 50th Birthday I started having vivid dreams featuring an Asian-looking elephant. On the third night, which was the eve of my birthday, the dream involved the smell of my grandma. Sounds odd, but my grandma always applied a pink cream called Germolene onto her legs as she suffered from psoriasis, and she always wore a perfume - well two – one was Lily of the Valley and another was called 4711. Then came one of my aunties who had passed a year or two before and she had with her an old flame she lived with when I was a young girl. I don't know much about him or how long they were together, but his name was Mathew and he was from Nigeria. My Auntie Edna had been in and out of my life a lot as a youngster, however, I wouldn't say we were particularly close. I was confused why she, of all, would show herself - still to remain a mystery.

Then as I lay there, I saw myself standing on stage talking publicly to a large room full of people with a book in my hands; a book I had written myself. Oh, I had also created a new online business that gave me the opportunity to work with women globally. "Wow" and "yeah right" I thought, nice dream but that came out of nowhere, I've never been one to have aspirations or goals, or even be career minded as such. I've always worked hard for what I have and that was whatever I needed to, to get by and pay the bills, then I was happy. So, not for a single minute did I think this was ever going to become a reality.

On the morning of my birthday, a good friend of mine had kindly offered to drive me to a place called Crystal Castle. I'd seen this on Facebook years ago and was wowed by the beauty of this amethyst cave. I hadn't realised until recently that it was in this country and in the next state, so I made it a bucket list item for myself. Having this opportunity to go on my 50th birthday was a big deal for me, and to make it even more special, I had booked a meditation session in the enchanted cave.

The cave was nothing how I imagined it would be. In fact, it has to be one of the weirdest encounters of my entire life. I arrived and filled in some paperwork, put on some safety gear and greeted the cave to welcome myself to it, by the girl who was giving a guided meditation. We were guided into the cave, did a 30 minute meditation laying in the cave, then thanked the cave for our presence.

As I lay there listening to this guided meditation, I found her voice starting to really annoy me, then for some reason the elephant returned. Then, without exaggeration, every single being I had ever met in my entire life flashed before me. I know it sounds unimaginable, but seriously I saw faces I'd forgotten, whether I chose to or not, then appeared three spiritual guides - one an ancient Egyptian who worked on the pyramids, one a native American Indian, and another one I'm unable to identify. Right there above me. I had the same flashes of me on stage again with the book and all of these wonderful attendees being inspired by me. Then I saw myself above me, looking back at me. I was having an out-of-body experience. I could literally see the confused expression on my own face laying there, then along came the elephant and gone, nothing.

I was awoken by some bells; we leave the cave and when the guide asked how it was and if it was it how I'd imagined, I blurted out all this confusion, which she said was amazing. How did I not feel amazing? I could hardly speak it out loud properly, I felt so emotional. She went over to where I was laying, pulled out a piece of amethyst that I had been laying on, and gifted it to me. I was in floods of emotional tears. It was an absolutely incredible experience!

I later learned that the elephant was Ganesh, the remover of obstacles. He is a God of Hinduism and the god of wisdom, success, and good fortune. And to top it off, when I got home my friend handed me a small gift as a keepsake and birthday reminder from the trip, I opened it and in amazement it was indeed a white carving of a Ganesh. I had not mentioned this nor seen them at the shop, so I was bewildered. He still takes a place of pride on my desk. Oh, and I have only had him appear to me in my dreams once since that day!

Going with the flow

Since this experience I have been open to what the universe has in store for me. I put all my trust and belief in her and although I have had to work a lot on self-doubt at times, I have reached way beyond any challenging comfort zones and I have still allowed myself to flow in the direction she leads me; the direction is my passion and my purpose. Because of this I have been following the signs that have been brought to me and studied courses, worked with spiritual teachers and life coaches, gained qualifications in spiritual life coaching, and signed up to write a book - this very book in fact. I have moved on from not only completely fully booking myself in my massage and holistic therapy business, I have managed to also create an expanding online and offline business. My entire world has exploded - I have unveiled the real me - and I'm not saying this has been an easy ride but it's certainly an encouraging and inspiring one that keeps me excited for what the future shall continue to bring me, now that I'm open to trust.

Sharing my gold

Being true to yourself and trusting yourself are big in their own right and I've always had the view that honesty pays, at whatever the cost to others. I'm sure you've heard the expression "truth hurts" and yes it most often does, but I'm one of those people who can handle what I know, it's always been the unknown I've struggled to handle, so I've had a life quest in search for the truth, one way or another.

Having said that, I have also spent a life lying, lying to the world, my family, my friends, colleagues, neighbours and anyone who came across me that didn't already know all the abuse and suffering that I held inside. All those memories and things I was too young to see, I held that up until recently. And yes, I was afraid that I may still hurt someone's feelings and I guarantee someone will try to call me out as they will feel shame and guilt. Well, I'm sorry they may feel inclined to do that, however, who was sorry back then? Who cared enough when I thought I needed it, who was ready to listen? But this is not to open up some kind of confessional or will for apologies, nor do I wish anyone to take the time now to try and rectify the past or justify their actions, it doesn't matter anymore, I've grown so far that I genuinely have gratitude to all those who contributed to the crap I've been dealt with.

All these experiences have moulded me into the strong and life-skilled woman that I am today. I'm proud of myself and to me that's all that counts. On this subject of trust, it hasn't always been easy to trust anyone and although I may have appeared on the surface to be open, giving and trusting, much of that was a front. I really was living a lie. I was two people; the one who allowed people to believe I was, and the tortured, untrusting one that I hid.

Part of me is sorry I had to lie all my life but what I'm not sorry for is using all that pain and keeping it locked away to protect myself, my vulnerability, for what I believed would be used against me somehow. I just never wanted to be seen as the girl that someone did blah blah blah to, or the, did you know she… girl. I wanted to be liked and treated like every other normal person I came across.

Ok, that's not really a thing is it? The older we get the more we realise we all have skeletons in our closet or fears, phobias, and we all have a past. We all grow into who we're meant to be, you just don't see that when you're in hiding and denial, until you finally allow the mask to slip away and trust that things were just the way they were for no apparent reason. I will add that having trust and belief that everything happens for a reason gives me the strength to take many more risks in life.

I'm not easily fazed, I take situations on board very lightly and I don't get offended easily. I'm what they call broad shouldered. A lot of my attitude can be attributed to the amount of very strong and opinionated women I had surrounding me in my family. My Grandma, God bless her, she was better known as the Welsh Dragon, and the matriarch of the family. I believe my mother now holds that title; being the first born. My Grandma was always the one who everyone went to and I believe I get that from her. Having spent a lot of my early years with her, that wouldn't surprise me.

With my Aunties, you always knew where you stood, and I admire that. Ok, I do have one Auntie who even today some relatives, if not all, are wary of what they say to her in fear of her response, but I admire her courage and openness to express her thoughts and opinions; she's always been my fave. The women she raised are so strong-willed and independent and this has followed down the generations. I see this in my own grandchildren now, so feistiness lives in each of us and certainly travels through our bloodline.

Life certainly has a lot to answer to, and we can make it easy or hard for ourselves. As I keep saying, it is us alone who chooses what we do and how we live in the end. I know circumstances and obstacles can and always will get in the way, and often defer the wishful direction, however, instead of allowing other people's beliefs and choices depict how you live your life, stop making excuses and do whatever it takes for you to live a carefree and wholesome life.

Visualisation

If you haven't used visualisation as a tool to see and feel the trusting person living the life you desire, I highly recommend you try it.

For anyone willing and trusting enough - I have one you could try just here.

Be sure to be alone. Maybe find some amazing meditation music; I'd suggest a binaural beat to reduce any anxiety and get more focus and clarity, as well as promote creativity during the sessions. If you want to dig deeper and with caution, I would suggest using subliminal beats to get that message in your brain subconsciously. This sends messages within the music, so you need to be selective when choosing the messages you want to get in and not fill your mind with negative or dangerous thoughts.

Laying down always works better for me, however, sitting comfortably upright with both feet flat on the ground is highly recommended as you're in position to raise your vibration and connection to the divine.

Eyes closed and relaxed, take in seven breaths. Breathe through your nose to the count of seven, hold it for seven, then breath out of your mouth for seven, holding again for seven, then repeat this seven times, concentrating only on the breath. Now I want you to imagine yourself still and calm, then a ball of bright blue light is situated in your tummy. This ball has warmth and a slight vibration that gives you a sense of awareness of protection.

As you lay there feeling at peace with yourself as you're safe and warm, the blue light ball starts to increase, and continues to increase, filling each and every cell of your body. As it fills your body you can imagine where it flows and how it feels. You should start to feel lighter and as if you're being wrapped up in a massive hug of love. This blue energy light ball will start to seep out of your body and fill the room you're in. Imagine everything it touches as you lay there, with your eyes closed. Imagine how all your furniture or whatever is surrounding you now has this beautiful bright blue haze of energy expanding further and further into the horizon and everything it touches becomes just how you would dream it to be. If you have bodily aches/pains/any emotions or feelings arising, just embrace them; allow yourself to love anything that comes into your mind right now.

If you can, try and replace in your mind how you're feeling about yourself and picture yourself as the happiest, healthiest, most vibrant version of yourself you possibly could. Each and every scar that is emotional and physical are just a massive part of the authentic you. How amazing you are, the only one in the world created like you. There is and can never be another one like you. That is incredible. You're free, you're safe from harm. You're surrounded by a protective shield from this moment on. You're adored, intelligent and confident, you feel alive. How carefree do you want to be? In your imagination right now that can be anything, just be sure you feel this.

Think about how you want your surroundings to look like; where in the world are you? What does your home look like? Is your sofa comfy? What colours have you decorated your personal space at home? How beautiful is your front garden? Is it grass, sand and ocean or maybe you love the paved or marbled front? This is your time to get really intricate and detailed in all you'd love around you. How comfortable and safe is your new home? Now what do you do for fun? Imagine all those wonderful adventures and activities you love to involve into your world.

Who is in your life? Do you have a loving, trusting, empathetic, fun, adventurous partner in your life who loves you unconditionally, who allows every single part of you to simply exist and shine? Are your family different towards you, now that you can guarantee they are honest to you and allow you to be yourself and love you just as you are? In your mind now is where you can have the life and the you that you really want. How does this feel?

I'm guessing you're feeling quite fabulous right now, so hold that feeling and emotion as the bright blue light decreases back towards you and slowly returns to a small ball of blue light in your tummy again. Now what you do with that ball of light is up to you. For me, I like to sit it in heart and let it evaporate into me at its own pace.

When you're ready you can slowly start to wiggle your fingers and toes, then bring some small movements back into your limbs. Take a few really nice deep breaths; remember in the nose and out the mouth. Open your eyes and have a drink of water.

That is one of my own visualisations. If you did decide to use this one, then I hope you got a sense of trust and belief that everything looks and feels better when you do have trust in your life.

What to do now

"How will I know if I can ever trust someone again, especially as I've been treated so badly?"

My response would have to be, if you want to regain any sanity then you need to learn to trust somewhere; you can't begin to move forward with your life until you do find trust, and that has to start with yourself. Trust your instincts and learn to trust your own decisions and begin by becoming familiar with and understanding your own vulnerabilities.

"I'll never trust another man for as long as I live."

This is like saying, "I'll never have another baby," once you've just given birth! Because trust or not, we still go ahead and get involved, don't we? I've been guilty of this so many times myself it's ridiculous; I've lost count. So, yes this is a tricky one and takes a lot of time. However, if you don't start believing there are trusting men out there then you're never going to meet one, not ever. Remember what I said about the energy we give off? Well this is no different, plus unless you're happy to continue having untrusting relationships, you'll be alone forever. I'm not saying that's necessarily a bad thing, but it's not for everyone, and certainly not myself, so maybe that's up for consideration. Once you do try and build up your own confidence and take the time discovering yourself, you'll be getting there.

"Who am I supposed to believe in now? My hopes and faith have been totally crushed?"

This was from a client feeling like she had been totally let down by her church, and afraid to move to another. So, I suggested that she needed to find her own supply of faith, whether it be God, the source, divine or any other higher good that she could rely on and build up her sense of belief and get that area supported somehow.

What can you take from this chapter?

Remember that trust is the basis around all human relationships and trusting someone means you think or believe they are reliable, you have confidence in them, and you feel safe - mentally physically and emotionally. Trust is built better with time, so please give yourself that.

Some tips to help you to trust yourself:

- ❖ Try the visualisation techniques.

- ❖ Be yourself and stop trying to be who you think others want you to be.

- ❖ Set a few reasonable goals for yourself and make sure you achieve them.

- ❖ Be kind to yourself. Being hard on yourself and forcing yourself to do something new isn't going to get you there any quicker.

- ❖ Learn your strengths, weaknesses and obstacles, then work on them. This is a toughie but it's also a great challenge for yourself.

- ❖ Spend some time alone. This is essential to get to know your own beliefs again and learn what it takes to enjoy you own space.

- ❖ Make some proud moments by creating some positive choices and reward yourself.

Some scientifically-proven ways to earn trust:

- ❖ Ask someone what you can give; have a look and see what is needed.

- ❖ Enjoy some meaningful conversation, or at least make an effort to talk to people around you.

- ❖ Offer some reassurance; letting people know you care can open up lots of potential for trust.

- ❖ Be honest with yourself and your own thoughts.

- ❖ Be loyal. Don't be a gossip. You'll be amazed how soon word gets around and I said before, if someone's talking about someone to you, then they're doing it about you too, so don't be that person.

- ❖ Remember you're only human, if you make mistakes, then own up to them, embrace them and learn from them. Yes, it's acceptable and even ok.

- ❖ Know who you are. Learn what your morals, standards and ethics are and please stick to them. Don't be a hypercritic - that's lying to yourself again and how can you trust a liar?

Back on the market - the dating game

The Australian national university (ANU) research has shown that 105 boys born for every 100 girls born (2017 stats)[4] so I doubt we're ever in a position of thinking they are all taken. There are plenty to go around, so what are you waiting for?

It may be surprising to learn that 2019 world statistics show that the United Nations (unstats.un.org), estimate there are 3,776,294,273 men – that's a shit load of males out there! And when you consider that there are 3,710,295,643 females, using the math = 65,998,630 more men in the world available for the taking.[5]

---

[4] ANU 2017

[5] Unstats.un.org

There are hundreds of dating statistics, including some fun ones, so here goes.

47.6% are women and 54% are men that date online, and 17% of them will end in marriage.[6] See there is hope for anyone wanting to commit again.

It only takes around 18 months of courtship before marriage from online dating opposed to a timeframe of 42 months if you date offline.[7] So, depending on how fast you want to move to marry again, there's your figures to work on! Wow, well ok I can personally beat this one - I was married at around six months from meeting my present husband online.

Although I could write an entire book on this subject, I'm going to try and minimise this into a chapter, so be prepared for the good the bad and the ugly, when it comes to the dating game. I say game because there are winners and a whole lot of losers, and you're going to have to be prepared for what's in store. I can't give you an accurate figure of how many dates I've been on, nor how many dating sites I've joined and scrolled through, as there have been so many. I've managed to make so many mistakes and learnings as I've seen the errors going from how to complete the profile through to choosing a date - the in-between is where it gets interesting.

You might be thinking your dating days are over – that you're scarred for life and will never trust another man for the rest of your life, or you believe you're too old and haven't got the energy to go there, or you're thinking who's going to want tried or damaged goods. Maybe you're a package deal so consider yourself out of range for a decent guy again, or just maybe all the good ones are married, gay or taken.

---

[6] Mantelligence.com

[7] Mantelligence.com

Back on the market - the dating game

Well, you couldn't be further from the truth. Look at the statistics above; have you seen how many men in the world there are right now?

Time will tell

If and when you do start dating again, let's look at the benefits. You get to meet a new man, or men, until you find one you gel with, it's a great excuse to get out the house again and socialise with another adult - one with the opposite sex to stimulate your mind amongst other stuff. After all, we're all women and we all have needs, whether that be mental, physical, sexual, emotional, or educational stimulation, and it's on each of you to decide what you need. Just remember, it's all available to you, plus you get to have some bloody well-earned fun again, even if fun is all you're looking for, as long as you can keep that clear in your mind/message/profile and conscious self, then that's fine. Keep it real and no one will get mixed messages; this is extremely important.

Getting out there again and socialising and having fun dates can bring you a whole new journey of adventures and experiences, especially if you're currently not leaving your home or safe environment anymore. Being able to open yourself to trying new experiences will inspire and educate you, so how valuable is that all just from dating?

Men have had different lives to us women and can teach us how to relax in ourselves or chill out to become more childlike sometimes and we all need this in our lives as we often allow life experiences to prevent us from allowing that part of us to emerge.

The good

Dating again will allow you to grow in yourself and discover what type of man you are wanting in your new life now, especially as you've spent a whole chunk of your life with another man. All the expectations you had or maybe still have will alter how you view yourself and any man you think you want in your future. So, use dating as an experiment to learn what you like and dislike now you've changed, now you're no longer the woman you used to be. Use dating as an opportunity to learn what you want in a relationship or work out if you are wanting a relationship or companionship at all.

Some funny stats about online dating

48% of 1000 women want a romantic man.[8] I'm in that category, however, I can confirm romance means different things to each of us.

26% of women believe in love at first sight.[9] I too have experienced this with my children's father.

93% of women prefer to be asked out on a date first. 6% like to ask a man first.[10] I'm not sure what happened to the remaining 1%!

These three stats taken from Mantelligence.com

So, what different types of dating are out there? And which type are you open to trying? Which one will suit your needs the most?

---

[8] Mantelligence.com
[9] Mantelligence.com
[10] Mantelligence.com

The profile

We have the most successful modern form known as online dating. I know this gets a lot of stick, and sometimes rightfully so, however, it has lots of absolutely amazing thumbs up reasons to start dating, or at least an introduction to the type of man you're actually looking for. My advice is to be absolutely clear on your profile about who you are and what you really are looking for.

Don't be making shit up about what you look like, do for a living, how old you are or what you love to do. If you lie here, you're not only lying to yourself, but you are going to attract a liar, or be deeply let down once the real you is unveiled, and it's such a valuable waste of everybody's time and energy. Secondly, be very focused on what you really want to achieve from the man you're going to be communicating with. Be certain you really do know who and what you want from a man. And look, I'm not saying he's got to look and act like Quasimodo but seriously height, weight and colour of hair should not be a priority, nor should the type of car he drives. Star signs I do understand! What you need to start off with is total honesty; be realistic too.

If you're looking for a fun date and nothing more, then that's what you apply for, and you can be picky and choosy about the superficial stuff. And what he does for fun, play around and seek out new adventures and conversations, let your hair down. Just don't expect Prince Charming to sweep you off your feet, but if it happens for you, then bonus. Also, there are many features that suit the modern-day women. In the safety of your own home you can ask the potential date anything you really want to know. All the questions you want or need, answers to questions that you may be a little nervous or shy to ask in person; use this as the time to find out. You can ask if he is married or has ever been married, then what went wrong, and look out for any red flags, please don't be too trusting straight away, treat this process as an interview.

You can ask if he's been convicted of a crime and if so, ask for details, and ask him how he feels about it now. Does he have any children? If not, how does he feel about children - does he want any or is he happy having children in his life? Ask if he has nieces and nephews, then listen about how he talks about them; this is a true indicator as to what type of man he really is. If he does have children, don't be afraid to ask how his relationship with them is - how often does he see them and what do they do with their time together. See how you're building a healthy picture of the real him? If he doesn't want to discuss this or other topics, politely move on to the next potential date until you find someone man enough to offer and share this information to you. Don't be fooled by the 'let's get to know each other first' line, because these are the 'let's get to know each other first' lines you want before you pass go.

Ask what his relationship with his parents and other family members is like. Ask about his friends. All of these questions may sound invasive, but hey this could be a guy you think looks amazing and his profile shows you the type of guy you've got in your head as the dream man, until you start unveiling the man behind the profile. I strongly advise you wait before meeting in person, and under no circumstances do you give your personal number, address or social media details until you're certain you haven't got a creepy stalker on the other end.

The bad

Men will tell you anything they believe you want to hear to meet you or get your details. And believe me, there are dating hackers and scammers out there; men claiming their undying love for you and really, they are not who they claim to be, giving false photos and names for profiles. Then usually they will make contact via email, text, Viber, Messenger, or WhatsApp just to take your money and never show up.

Back on the market - the dating game

I could tell you at least five stories of women I have met who have paid out a ridiculous amount of money to men, apparently helping them to arrange to fly to them or to set up a home together, or to help pay off a debt or pay the ex-wife off to free them for you. These poor ladies were taken advantage of while in a vulnerable state and lost thousands of pounds or dollars to these men who prey on all of you. They have vulnerable woman radars. I beg you not to judge these ladies, they are not at fault here, only guilty of being fooled by the need to love and be loved.

Believe it not, we throw out 'come and get me' vibes and they smell us a mile off, as do narcissists and psychopaths, so this is why I ask you to ask all the bloody questions first, and still be aware of the rest. This goes for drunken meets - seriously how many of you have gone out on a fabulous girl's night out, work party or even a holiday, had a few too many and thought you'd pulled a cracker, to wake up in the morning with regrets? I'm sure we've all encountered a drunken date or kiss or even a cheeky dance haven't we, so we know how that feels. Ok, it may feel fabulous at the time, but it's not the answer. Often women take these men back to their own homes or rooms and there are horror stories to be told here too. How do you know the man you've pulled and decide you want a one-night stand with isn't a rapist or a murderer? You don't. They really aren't all that bad though; there's some yummy men in the bars when you have your beer goggles on!

Going on a blind date

Blind dates can be fun. Getting fixed up can swing either way; your friends or colleagues could genuinely know a guy that you'd fit very well with, or they have a desperate pal, brother or colleague they want off their backs, or they are fed up of you turning up to all the couple's occasions alone so feel obliged to match you up with the single brother or neighbour. So many stories spring to mind right now. I've been that single girl where friends thought it was funny to fix me up. In fact, after my second marriage failed, my best friend and I decided it was time for me to have a bit of fun, so arranged us to meet at her husband's birthday party. The alcohol kicked in and I admit, I'm not a very good drunk, however, her husband's friend was so comical he had me laughing for hours, and you know what us women are like when a man can make us laugh. We both only wanted a bit of fun, but that one night stand lasted eight years. Like I said, be careful of blind and drunk dates!

Speed dating

I've never tried it before but I quite like the fun concept of speed dating. Actually, I've done plenty of speed dating - they've been over so fast I've forgotten I was on one! Seriously though, the idea of sitting in a room with a number and everyone experiencing the same person to talk to and check out is amazing, is in a safe environment, plus you can feel the energy instantly. You can watch the body language and have a sneak at how they act when leaving the last table. And you don't even need to see or speak to any of them again should you not want to. That's all I know on that, apart from the scene in the movie Hitch!

Darkness dating

Oooh, in the dark dating, where there's a dark room full of people and you don't know what they look like but you get to hear each other and talk without being seen. I'm not sure if you can touch or not, but in the movie "The Notebook" they enter a dark room dating event and that's the only time I've come across that. I see the benefits and the dangers in this one.

Singles clubs

Oh, bring on the singles clubs and singles bars with events! Again, I haven't participated, but I know of a few that been around for a lot of years, let me tell you. It's great as some online dating sites will provide their own events for singles where you can meet up with or without the guys you've already connected with through the site, or just mingle and see if you connect with anyone, and as you're all there for the same purpose, I'm sure they are safe. Unless you've turned up at a swinger's bar or party, then either drop your keys in a basket or run like crazy! Oh, in case you're wondering, the answer is no, I haven't, however, one of my exes – who I won't name - tried to push me in this direction. I'm afraid that sharing my man with another woman, or being fondled or more by another man in front of my own is not my cup of tea. My motto was always, "I don't mess around, but I don't hang around", meaning I may not be unfaithful, but I will quickly move onto another relationship. Well that was my past, now I know what I know, my whole dating and relationship attitude has changed dramatically, thankfully.

A random meet

So now that leaves us with the good old fashioned and traditional way of meeting or dating - leaving it to destiny, bumping into a stranger and hitting it off, going to a library or museum, maybe a hobby club, gym, maybe someone in your workplace or a chance meet up. This means do not plan or expect anything, just allow and be.

My final online dating match

My daughter decided she wanted me to come to Australia a year earlier than I had planned and wanted me to find love in Australia. I was happy on my own with a very good FWB (friend with benefits) as and when it suited us. I wasn't looking for a permanent relationship. However, she took it upon herself to create a dating profile looking for a suit for her mum. I know that can sound desperate, but it wasn't put that way! I had quite a lot of interest and my daughter kept sending me pictures of profiles but I was like no, no, no hell no!

So, eventually I came around and started talking to three guys. They were all nice in their own way, but I soon eliminated one so that left two., I tackled back and forth before eventually choosing the one, he was a guy I would never have chosen before. What led me to him - well he was direct, raw and adventurous. So, for me he wasn't going to tell me something I wanted to hear, nor pretend to be something he wasn't, nor was he superficial, nor built with high expectations. He had been through some tough times himself and I listened to my intuition this time. So, we started online dating, which quickly moved to Facebook and Messenger. Remember, I am in England and he is in Australia.

We continued to grow our relationship by making daily video calls and we involved each other's friends and family. So, we had a real-life relationship without the touch and smell of each other.

It worked. So, we decided I needed to come sooner rather than later, six months later as it happened. I decided to sell up, leave my life in England and risk it all. So, I made the commitment and travelled to Australia on a visitor's visa in October 2016, just days before my birthday. We went travelling together for around three months and saw some beautiful destinations. It didn't take long before I realised he wouldn't suit the English lifestyle, so it became apparent that we would live our life together here in Australia. So, three months later we were married in a little park and we haven't been apart since, except for the odd work commitment of course.

We now live in a beautiful part of the world in Australia and we have increased our animal family with our dog, Barney and parrot,

Horus. My life with him has allowed me to evolve as myself through lots of self-development and Geoff's Australian laid-back attitude gave me time to totally be myself and create this amazing life and business where I am able to give so much back. I have to say this is the first time in my life I feel complete happiness and carefree. I have my bliss.

The ugly

The dating downside is you're likely to meet a load of dickheads and idiots, which has the potential to put you off men for longer, if not life. Whether you choose online or offline, all the rules apply. Be honest, be aware, be true and be safe. You really don't have to be alone; I wouldn't want anyone being sad or lonely and end up depressed because they are afraid to look for happiness again. Nor do I want you spending hours and hours scrolling through the many dating apps and still not find your Mr Right. The last thing I want is you to create a stressful experience full of anxieties and triggers for yourselves, through choosing or waiting, when dating can bring you so much joy and fun. If you really are insistent on a solo life and you're content and full of joy, then that too can bring many a positive outcome and a healthy future for you. After all, this is your life and it's your choice how you live it.

To prove my point - there is someone out there for everyone, yes, even you. I have created a program that allows you to learn who you are, what you're looking for in a partner or date, and how to consciously go through the dating process and find the best way to date for you. Plus if it is online, how to set up and work through a dating site honestly and openly.

What to do now

"Where do I start dating?"

Well I always ask if you're really ready to take that step first. If not, then I highly recommend you take up my rapid recovery program first, otherwise another relationship will fail before you've even given it a chance to get going.

"It's been so long since I've had a date, I don't think anyone will want an old has-been like me".

Bless the many over 40's who think this is true, but it's so far from the truth, because you are never over the hill or too old. I know many women in their 60's and 70's still finding true love and having the time of their lives. You're never too old and it's never too late to start, and as long as you're breathing, you're able to still date and have fun.

"Where do I find a date these days"?

Well, as I've expressed earlier, there are plenty of opportunities, and lots of different dating methods, such as online dating sites with apps, your friends, family and colleagues arranging meet-ups or blind dates. Speed dating, singles clubs, workplaces or events, the local gym, coffee shops, libraries, a place of hobby, local events, a volunteer group, you name it there are opportunities absolutely everywhere around you.

Dating sites to suit all needs

Zoosk has been named #1 in the world, plus there's eHarmony, Elite Singles, Plenty of Fish, Tinder, Match.com, Adultfriendfinder, and many more. Explore, safely.

You can check out how to start working with me on this through my website. www.manifestmerriment.com

This is you

"Love yourself in your own skin and embrace your avatar!"

Zelda Marsh

"Knowing who you are is one of the greatest wisdoms a human being can possess. Know your goals, what you, your morals, your needs and your standards are, what you will tolerate and what you're willing to die for, it defines who you are."

Beyonce Knowles

There is no one, nor ever will be anyone more perfect than you. You are simply one of a kind, a perfectly unique and amazing soul living in human form and should be living life how only you know how. This, darling, is you.

How prepared are you to start living?

Only you can decide what your future looks like. By now you should have a clear idea of how you don't want to live it. Have you worked out what you're passionate about yet? Thought about everything you appreciate and love and how that fits into your world? Have you ever taken the time out to invest in yourself or work with someone to help you to learn who you really are? If not, then you need to get cracking. Sometimes we need a kick start to bring us into the present, pause, have a think about all of those areas and work out where you fit in the world and who you really are.

After all, if you are one of us who's had so many traumatic or lifechanging experiences such as a divorce, then you have to connect with who you've found and remember to disconnect with the past you; the one version of you that has long gone. Once you get there, you are going to be so freaking free and happy, living your life full of gratitude and joy. You'll not spare a minute for those miserable moments of the past to take you away from the life you deserve. Go and get your bliss, it's well worth the effort, that is for certain. Take a risk on your own happiness, even if it's the only risk you're prepared to ever take again. Do it, and experience for yourself what true and inner love really feels like.

Remember, you are who you are, don't you ever forget that. It's simple if not easy to just accept it, because until you do no one else will.

If you don't take action and accept your beautiful selves, you'll succumb to being co-dependant and never gaining your own voice. With that brings low self-esteem, self-doubt and a lack of confidence, plus you'll remain stuck behind that mask of pretence, constantly living a lie, with the potential to be miserable and sad, allowing depression to strike you, all because you're just not being true to yourselves.

What will it take to wake you up?

I had to lose everything to get my wake-up call. I don't want that for you and I don't recommend waiting for it to go that far either, however, that was what it took for me before I recognised what I needed. Once I had realised it, I made the choice to stand up and take action for myself. I found freedom and loads of time on my hands, which I used to not only think about myself and digest what I'd been through and what I could do to get myself feeling ok again, but to discover many wonderful locations and people. Only then I woke up to see what I did actually enjoy, and yet again this made me realise all the things I actually didn't like too. I would never have known this had I not had all that time alone. I'm not suggesting for a minute you need to run off to find yourself, although I'm not ruling that out if that suits you. I am saying take the time to get to know what you want, instead of like me and only knowing what you don't want and doing nothing about it for all those years.

Investments

The biggest shock for me came much later. I made the decision to care for myself once and for all, so I totally invested in myself by working with some amazing spiritual business coaches. While I was going through some self-development work, I chose to see what would naturally manifest towards me. Ironically, that's when everything started coming together. I knew I needed to experience how professionally coaching others worked, and me simply being qualified wasn't enough; I like to know what it feels like being on the other end of any treatment, and as I was to go out and do this role as part of my purpose, it made perfect sense.

Wow, I can't even put into words how life-expanding it is to be asked questions you've never said out loud before. Talk about make you think. I wasn't prepared for all the emotional outburst and awareness that opened me up to.

At times I became a child again, and I went through many trauma and tantrums as I continued through my life journey. I needed a whole lot more healing work to keep me going through this emotional rediscovery and I couldn't believe that all this time, effort and work I thought I had spent thinking I knew who I was, turned out to be just a smidge of me, in fact, I wasn't even close.

It is with much love and gratitude to my coaches, spiritual teachers and healers for guiding me through some traumatic healing and repressions, plus all their patience, love and teachings. I truly believe I owe them so much more, because they really did give me my self-aware and reflective new life. So, all this hands-on experience and pain has allowed me a greater understanding on a much deeper level to how many of my clients were to feel once we get to the nitty gritty.

I battled with discovering my niche for some time and I too resisted the notion of being able to serve all you amazing women out there. I can assure you I no longer have any doubts and just so you know, it's never really about the divorce anyway. These amazing people in my life saw me in a way I couldn't; ironically it has always been one of my gifts, being able to see and draw out the best in others, yet my own self-doubt prevented me seeing my own worth.

Self-love

So, what do I do for myself now to love, care and nurture, you may ask? Plenty! I take my diet and fluid intake very seriously; I'm a huge believer in you are what you eat, and food will heal itself given the right source. I don't eat meat nor dairy, I try to stay away from any processed foods and sugar is minimal. I'm still human and my naughty foods are battered fish and chips and mushy peas every so often, and jelly snakes are my downfall as are any other sweets when I'm in the mood. I have become a lover of juicing my own fruits and vegetables and I create superfood smoothies and bliss balls most days. I even make my own almond milk at times. I try to keep it as raw as possible. I drink plenty of water, herbal teas and very rarely touch alcohol.

Exercise is imperative now that I have been diagnosed with moderate osteoarthritis, and menopause to top it off! However, I choose to live medication-free, so I need to move regularly; for me it's the pool, reformers Pilates and barre fusion, and I get myself out in nature as often as I can. This could be a walk barefooted on grass and even hug a tree or two; don't knock it until you've experienced it! I'll walk on the beach near the water and will dip my toes in whenever possible, and yes, I've been known to run in fully clothed!

I meditate daily and as you would have already discovered I use Ho'oponopono, the ancient Hawaiian prayer daily. I have moments of play with my pets, Barney our Jack Russell Terrier and Horus my galah parrot. I love my children and my ever-increasing grandchildren, and my work, as I meet some amazing people all over the world. I feel like I have more friends now than ever in my life. I don't feel like I have a job at all. And I get so much back from what I do that I'm inspired to turn up over and over again and keep giving. Not to mention the networking - I'm now heavily involved and proud to be associated with some powerful and very empowered and inspirational businesswomen and men. And I am learning something new every day.

I have an amazing social life with some beautiful ladies, as well as my husband of course. I have hobbies that bring out my creative edge, from sewing group to walking and coffee groups. I feel like the world is my oyster. I am truly free and content with everything. I am grateful for every living day and I now seize every opportunity that feels right for me. I most certainly listen to my intuition all the time now. And I just love something every day of my life. Being and living in my own identity has been a long time coming and I am now excited about where my future journey will take me.

I want each and every one of you readers to feel this in your life too, and you can if you allow yourself to just love yourself.

What to do now

"I am happy as I am, I don't need to change."

I sincerely hoped this was the case for this client, however, as I explained to her, she had just come away from a divorce and had to move away from her lovely home, so she had already changed but at the time wasn't aware of it, the life and the person she had grown into. However, there is no going back, you cannot undo you, but you can adapt or change the you that you are now into, whoever and however you feel happy with, but still change is change and inevitable.

I really felt sorry for the lady who had been trodden on emotionally in her relationships all her life, that all she could think of was no-one would like who she really was, so was happy living behind her mask to keep people happy. I had to step in and say how sorry I was that she felt like that way, but to be true to herself it was, "Tough titties. I'm sorry, but how people view you is on them, not you, it's none of your damn business what goes on in their lives any more than it is what goes in yours. Besides anyone who is meant to be in your life will be. Yes, you may lose a few of those so-called friends or colleagues or even family members, but don't worry you'll attract the people that are meant to have in your life to fit you."

"Will I ever discover who I'm meant to be?"

Good question and absolutely, yes of course you shall, if that's what you really want of course. I quickly introduced this client to one of my programs and with some strategies and tools that she followed, mostly keeping on track, she succeeded to where she wanted to be at that time. Even I was amazed at her results.

This is you

She totally reconnected with herself and I'm so proud of how this beautiful woman grew in front of my eyes.

There is room in our years to find our own happy place; my wish is that each and every one of you reading this book right now finds total bliss.

Now go and reclaim your own passion and purpose. Find the way to love yourself unconditionally, as I do. I love you.

A little task to get you started:

- ❖ Write down 20 things you love about yourself.

- ❖ Name 10 things you are grateful for in your life.

- ❖ Write down 5 future goals you'd like to achieve and next to each item write what you're going to do about it.

I'd like to end this book with a beautiful song by an incredibly talented lady, Kaela Settle, singing her amazing, touching and captivating theme from 'The Greatest Showman," *This is me.*

This sums me up as it is all about being proud and brave by standing out as yourself and loving it.

BE YOU-BE LOVE-BE TRUE-BE HAPPY-BE FREE-BE YOUR OWN POWER

Testimonials- Continued

There is so much I can say about Zelda, I don't know where to start. To begin with, she is and has been one of the greatest friends one could ask for. Truly, she has been known to be there for me when she has sometimes needed the same support herself. She has never let me down, always has the knack to make me smile. I couldn't be more than thankful to have her in my life, I miss her every day, especially when I need someone to talk to.

Zelda has had many hardships in her life that she has overcome, and it has made her a fighter, a very hard worker. One of Zelda's best qualities is that she listens and is able to see from all points of view in any situation.

Gemma Collis
Grimsby
England

At the young age of 16 I had a mundane job as a fish packer; a rather boring role done on a daily basis. That was until one day I was put opposite an unusual soul who reminded me of a witch, with her dark hair and big eyes. I asked her name; I couldn't believe it when she told me it was Zelda - no way was she actually named after a witch! She then told me her parents named her after a dog. I laughed my head off and that was the start of a beautiful friendship. Zelda became my mentor and best friend, we shared so many happy years together and through our younger years we managed to have five children between us. There have been times in our friendship that we have been separated due to work commitments and the men in our lives, but I have always known that if ever I needed her she would be there and vice versa, and it would always feel like we last spoke yesterday.

Zelda is an amazing, wonderful person and I am very honoured to have her in my life as a lifelong friend - I'll love her always.

Victoria Atkinson
Queen's Cleans
Cleethorpes
England

I have known Zelda for many years now, firstly meeting through work then to become good friends. You could not ask for anyone more loyal, friendly, hardworking and loving, it doesn't matter what she may be going through herself, she will always make time and be there for other people, putting her own life on hold for others. Zelda came and stayed with me and my family when she was going through one of the most difficult times of her life. With a little encouragement she made it through and came out a much stronger and confident lady. Zelda has one of the most infectious laughs

Testimonials-Continued

and she loves life, her friends and her family. Anybody who has Zelda in their lives are richer for having her. There is nothing that makes me happier than seeing her so settled and happy now, apart from my selfish part that wishes she hadn't had to go to the other side of the world to find the life she deserves.

Elizabeth Downing
Owner/Manager Agent Smart LTD
Denholme
England

Zelda, you are one of the most positively energised people I know. You sprinkle your magic upon all those that come into contact with you. Your energy is bright and colourful and you have a beautifully natural way of being able to connect with others and allow them to Just Be. You are a rainbow that shines brightly in this busy place we call life. You make a difference to others simply by being you. As you weave your way through this life you will leave those that need a little something all the better to have crossed your path.

Deb Wiseman
Brisbane, Qld, Australia

Author Bio

Zelda Marsh 'escaped' from the north-eastern town of Grimsby in England to consciously create a brand-new life for herself in the beautiful Queensland suburb of Redcliffe in Australia after - in her own words - she 'hit the pits,' leaving everything she knew behind her.

Zelda worked herself up to a management position within her career in the health and social sector, and this, along with her holistic therapies, she believes has moulded her morals and ethics with her love for people and understanding the needs of vulnerable adults.

Within three years of her new life, she has remarried and is now the founder of 'Manifest Merriment'. She has qualified as a Holistic, Beauty and Sports Therapist, and has now embarked on a continued path as a Spiritual Life Coach, specialising in working with women after divorce with her successful Rapid Recovery Program.

BounceBackAbility

Zelda Marsh has lived an unstable life of chaos, abuse, neglect and violence, yet has always maintained the ability to bounce back with a smile, her incredible sense of humour and a positive outlook on life. She puts this down to her strength and spiritual guidance.

She claims her title as an expert in her field because she has extensive life skills to support it. These include being the child of divorced parents, going through two divorces, and being a victim of domestic violence, alongside other turbulent and unhealthy relationships. She is a proud mum to her three gorgeous children and has eight grandchildren - so far.

You will find Zelda somewhat unique in her practices. She prides herself on her ability, using her innate intuition, to just 'know' what the deep issues really are. She is approachable, friendly, warm and loving, with an authentic openness that draws you in with her magnetising energy.

More about Zelda and her work can be viewed on www.manifestmerriment.com

Get a peek at....
A bite sized freebie of this Ebook created to give you a taster of how life goes on.

As my gift to you

GET IT HERE
http://bit.ly/freeEbookafterdivorce

Are you lonely?
Are you bitter or angry?
Do you lack high self-esteem?
Still struggling to let go of your ex after your divorce?

Are you searching for love and don't know where to start?

If you answered yes or can relate to any of the above, then this offer is for you.

- 30 minute connection call

- A full one-on-one session to unveil the truth behind the loneliness or bitterness

- Unlimited access to a private Facebook group for women after divorce

- An insight into the Rapid Recovery Program and an eligibility test

Rapid Recovery session normally $250 Book offer - quote BounceBackAbility offer only $49

Contact Zelda Marsh-
zeldamarsh.coach@gmail.com
www.manifestmerriment.com

Notes

BounceBackAbility

Notes

BounceBackAbility

Notes

www.ingramcontent.com/pod-product-compliance
Lightning Source LLC
Chambersburg PA
CBHW021436080526
44588CB00009B/556